MW01610148

God
I'm Busy

**Escape Busyness and Distractions
to See God's Awesome Faithfulness**

Alan Bias

Book cover design and book layout Omar Mediano
www.omarmediano.com

Front cover page turn design Lomy Chiv
lomy@lomychiv.com

Front cover black and white photograph
© Michael Blamey
www.todaymelbourne.blogspot.com
www.stkildatoday.blogspot.com

Book cover color photographs
© Laura Ann Sorrell

ISBN 978-1-4276-5204-1

For more information and book orders, please visit:
www.GodImBusy.com

Steps of Hope
P.O. Box 863624
Plano, TX 75086
972-758-1260

God I'm Busy
Escape Busyness and Distractions to See God's Awesome Faithfulness

Acknowledgment v

Preface vii

1. So What's the Problem? 1

2. The Good the Bad and the Ugly of My Journey . . . 17

3. Turn Off, Tune In, Hear God 37

4. Our Perception of Time 53

5. How Memory Works 69

6. What Is The Big Gray Swirl? 81

7. Escaping The Big Gray Swirl 93

8. Practical Suggestions and Coaching 115

9. Conclusion 123

Appendix One 125
   A Few Scriptures About the Faithfulness of God

Appendix Two 131
   Testimonies of Escaping The Big Gray Swirl

Appendix Three 143
   A Vision of the Future

Acknowledgment

It has been said that Beethoven could hear a piece of music in his head and simply write it down. For me, however, the process of writing this book was far from simply hearing from God and writing it down. Over the past year while writing this book, I've become more aware of God's faithfulness than ever before.

My wife and her strength to endure this process has been the single greatest manifestation of God's faithfulness in my life. Although I don't believe in overly celebrating our bruises verses celebrating our victories, this past year has been difficult. During this time our family has been stretched more than ever before. My wife has been as supportive as anyone could possibly be. She patiently listened to me talk on-and-on about every concept, thought and story in this book. She gently suggested, "Maybe you can keep working on that part", when I wrote something awkwardly. She prayed for me and encouraged me. But most of all, she heard from God, trusted God and believed in me.

Next to my wife my children have also been fantastic. They have followed my wife's example wonderfully. Many nights they came into my office one after the other to kiss me goodnight and say, "I hope your book is going well. I'm praying for you."

There are so many other people who have been so helpful and wonderful. I am forever grateful and would love to try and name them all; however, I really want the focus of this acknowledgment to be on my wife and kids.

Johann Sebastian Bach said, "Music's only purpose should be the glory of God and the recreation of the human spirit." Recreation in Bach's day was regarded as relief from toil or suffering. I pray this book will be music for all who read it.

Thank you!

Preface

How This Book Will Help You

What if it were true that God has been very active in your lives, intervening on your behalf, blessing you, and speaking to you, but you either didn't hear it or couldn't remember it? For the majority of you this is true. You need to be freed from something you didn't even know had you captive. You need to be freed from *The Big Gray Swirl*.

The Big Gray Swirl is a culture of busyness in an environment of distractions which distorts your perception of time and prevents you from fully recognizing or remembering the words, experiences, and directions from God.

The result is weakened faith and very few if any stories of God's faithfulness have been recorded and ready to pass along to your children and grandchildren.

I will show you that while you're capable of hearing and remembering your interactions with God, your high speed, high tech culture is usually preventing you from doing so. The more you fail to hear or remember your experiences with God, the more likely you will experience doubt and unbelief. If when you go through tough times, you do not recognize and chronicle the faithfulness of God in the midst of your difficulty, you will tend to get frustrated, bitter, fearful and depressed. You will recall and relive your wounds rather than your victories. Additionally, you will not have those experiences, ready to pass along to your children to strengthen their faith.

As ridiculous as it first seemed, scientists eventually proved black holes *do* exist. They did it by proving where light should be seen in space but nothing was there. Likewise, there is a level of faith and intimacy with God we should experience and share with others that isn't there. I will show you the unseen reason why.

BUSYNESS AND DISTRACTIONS

If life seems to be flying by and you are rushing around fighting distractions with little time for recognizing God in the midst of your day and certainly no method for easily recalling all the times God specifically interacts with you, then you're caught in *The Big Gray Swirl*. If you follow the suggestions in this book, they will change your life significantly.

GENERATIONAL TRANSFER

Once your life begins to calm down, with less rushing around and fewer distractions, you will be ready to start depositing stories in your "faith bank" for the purpose of passing them on to your children. I call this a generational transfer.

All too often when we speak of an inheritance, we are speaking of money, property or material things. I inherited my grandmother's bibles and books. While I value my grandmother's bibles and books, I don't have stories of her experiences and life-lessons, in her own words. That would be a priceless heirloom I would own, hold and pass along to my children and grandchildren.

We read the stories of Jonah and the whale, David and Goliath, Gideon's army and Jericho. Those stories reveal the nature of God, because they are scripture. Having said that, I envision a day when along with those stories, children will have books of their parents' and grandparents' stories of God's faithfulness in their time.

I am creating a simple, easy-to-use tool for better capturing your victories, life-lessons and stories of God's faithfulness. I discuss this tool at the end of the book in appendix three, entitled, *A Vision of the Future.*

Book Synopsis

This book begins by discussing the basic problems of busyness and distractions in your life. It will then further your understanding of the problem while giving you examples of my own many personal struggles to become free, and enjoy a greater relationship with God than I ever thought possible. Next, you will discover the fascinating phenomenon of perceived time vs. actual time. Plus, how the memory works relative to your ability to remember God's interactions in your lives. The various threads of the book will be tied together as your eyes are opened to the biggest challenge of experiencing the awesome faithfulness of God while living in the 21st century. At this point, the book will provide you with a road map on how to escape *The Big Gray Swirl* along with simple, practical, everyday suggestions. The appendixes of the book shares scriptures about the faithfulness of God, testimonies of some individuals who have been set free, and my vision for the future.

Chapter 1

So What's the Problem?

Many of us end up with a sour attitude and bitter outlook on life because we've been dragged through trial after trial in our struggle to live well and follow God. We're exhausted by unending and numerous demands that leave us in a wake of gnawing disappointments, blistering frustration, and even numbing depression. And yet, we must admit that we're still here! In every trial, somehow we managed to live and maybe, if we're honest, even tasted something sweet in that which seemed entirely bitter. We can come to realize that while our days may be indeed tender with pain and seasoned by struggle, they are sweetened by God's faithfulness.

However, for those who never recognize God's divine interactions, those brief and seemingly quiet communications, life will be poisoned with fear and bitter foreboding. But to those who savor God's persistent presence, who can recall and quietly reflect on those interactions, life will be sweet with the realization of His love and His faithfulness.

EVERYONE IS BUSY

Can you honestly remember the last time you did not *feel* busy? My observations of the speed of life have led me to many conclusions, the least of which is that, as participants in this culture of busyness, we have far more to lose in the way of opportunities and moments than we could ever possibly hope to gain. And the things we stand to lose will not so much be lost as they will be missed as we go rushing by.

One man I met, the most unlikely person to be trapped in this gray swirl of busyness, showed me just how far reaching is this phenomenon of high speed life. On this particular day, I had planned to use my charge card at the grocery store and, therefore, was carrying not one bit of change when a homeless man standing by the front entrance approached me. Whether he expected an explanation or not as to why my pockets were empty, I offered one anyway. Then I proceeded to try and chat with him, inquiring as to his situation and how long he'd been on the streets.

Clearly agitated at my uninvited attempt at conversation, the man basically said, "Look, either give me some money or not because I gotta go!" I was standing there thinking about what he had said and I just had to ask, "Where? Where do you gotta go? You're homeless. How can you be busy?" The man explained that a church across town would be serving up dinner in about an hour and a half and he hoped for at least fifteen minutes more of pan handling time before starting the hour walk it would take him to get there. He was busy and he had every upcoming minute accounted for. I let him finish and then I made him an offer. I told him I would take him home, cook him dinner, and talk to him about how he could improve his situation.

He agreed so I took the man to my home, cooked him dinner, and grilled a couple of burgers for him to take on the road. He said his name was Thomas. I talked to Thomas about taking the first morning bus over to a transitional housing program. I offered to let him stay for the night to ensure he'd go but he chose, instead, to return to the grocery store so he could catch the bus first thing in the morning from there. After dinner, I drove him behind the grocery store and helped him stack and arrange some wooden pallets where there was a little space in the middle that wasn't visible from the outside. When we finished, he crawled right up in it and prepared to go to sleep, promising he'd make it over to the housing program.

A couple of days passed and I received an email from Thomas. Thankfully, he had been accepted into the program and had an email address as well as a physical address. In his email he invited me to attend church with him that coming weekend.

It was really amazing to me that even Thomas, a homeless man, had been caught up in busyness.

Because Thomas had slowed down long enough to come to dinner and because we discussed the option of a transitional housing program, he now, hopefully, had chosen the path to changing his life; but he almost missed this opportunity. In fact, he was ready to miss this opportunity because he was so busy rushing around. Not only that, but because he had not expected God to actively intervene in his life, he had not recognized an opportunity when it stared him in the face. You see, life is often made up of missed opportunities and life-changing moments that keep us trapped in the same rut year after year.

If you can't recognize when God is using people, situations, thoughts, and even nature to speak to you, how will you ever realize He cares about you and loves you? Likewise, even if you do experience God's interruptions in your day but get so distracted by demands that leave you exhausted at the end of the day, do you remember what He said? If you can't remember what God said, how will you ever get from Point A to Point B in life and worse, how will you ever be able to pass along those stories and rich truths to the next generation?

WHAT GRANDMA KNEW
ABOUT MICROWAVES

I often refer to our society today as a *microwave society*. My definition of a microwave society would be a society with little or no patience, and I mean little or no patience for anything. The biblical definition of patience (as paraphrased by me) is, "How long you are willing to deal with other people, your circumstances or God without getting frustrated and angry."

Now, thanks to the technology of instant communication and instant information, our microwave society has evolved into a high-speed microwave society. Some of us live in a constant state of frustration and anger. Our perception is, we don't have time for this, we don't have time for that and we really don't have time for the other. But can we change our perception of time so that it works in our favor and, if so, how do we do it?

Will changing our perception of time help us calm down and eliminate the overwhelming anxiety we feel over never having enough time?

The truth is we can find ways to slow down if we're intentional about it and keep our priorities straight. There are simple ways to do this that won't sabotage your life.

My grandmother hated the microwave. I still remember this although it's been many years. To her, the microwave represented negative shifts in simple but important behaviors. Over at our house, of course, the microwave enjoyed a happy life with a busy and appreciative family.

One summer my grandmother came to stay with us for two weeks while my parents chaperoned the high school band in Europe. At first, she quietly observed our behavior, watching us kids run in and out all day long, grabbing things from the freezer and the fridge, tossing them into the microwave, gulping them down, and running back out the door. This lasted for about one week before she finally said, "That's it! No more microwave. If you don't have time to cook food the right way, sit down for a bit and eat it, then you don't have enough time to eat. You need to just get on with whatever it is you're in such a big hurry over."

From that moment on, we'd come in, ask my grandmother for something to eat, chat with her while she fixed it for us, and then chat with her while we ate. Amazingly, we discovered that my grandmother had some really good input and advice about whatever it was we were doing at the time, whether it was a sport or a game or something else. Without being forced to be "fully present" with my grandmother for those short periods of time throughout the day, we would certainly have missed out on some very special moments and insights.

You see, rushing around everywhere robs us of our ability to truly be fully present in the here and now. I think my grandmother was able to intuitively see this.

We're being conditioned by our culture to accept in ourselves and accept in others this constant rushing around and busyness.

WHAT BUSYNESS COST COWBOY BOB

A while back there was a businessman who God had given me a heart for. I'll nickname him Cowboy Bob the Businessman. I would ride shotgun with Cowboy Bob once or twice a month, all day, just talking to him about the things of God. Now, Cowboy Bob was the ultimate "running-90mph-with-your-hair-on-fire" kind of guy and he drove like a madman. One day, as we were flying down the road from one meeting to the next, I actually counted five tasks that he was attempting to perform simultaneously. He was driving, reprogramming his GPS, eating a sandwich, chatting with his wife on a hands-free phone, and sporadically talking on a company phone to his guys in the field. At one point, he actually looked over at me and said, "I'm living life in the fast lane, Baby!" I thought, "You're doing something all right but I'm not sure what."

When we would arrive at a meeting, he'd say, "Let's go!" and he was always excited. However, because he was never really fully present during those meetings, I would often notice that he would miss much of the meeting's important nuances. After many meetings, I'd try to explain to Cowboy Bob that I could sense some frustration coming from his clients, but he would always say, "Oh, they'll be all right!"

During the times that Cowboy Bob and I rode together, I can remember countless moments when he expressed great surprise at the way certain things went wrong in his life. It was during these times that he'd question the faithfulness of God. When I'd try to explain just how much of life he was really missing due to his constant rushing around, when I would point out his distractions and his insistence on trying to fit a million things into one day, he'd dismiss me by recounting a story from his most recent vacation or by bragging proudly about his newest flat screen TV or about another of his large purchases.

What Cowboy Bob was essentially doing in response to my observations was pointing to his *money* as if, somehow, the answers lie therein. Sadly, when all was said and done Cowboy Bob ended up alone, with nothing but his money.

He was too busy to be concerned with all the little seemingly insignificant and trivial details of what he was doing and what it was doing to him.

So what's the difference if you microwave some-thing and eat it on the run verses taking a few minutes to use the stove and have a conversation with your spouse? What's the big deal?

I'M NOT DISTRACTED, I'M MULTI-TASKING

You may say, "Look at what the technology rev olution has done for us! Hasn't it simplified our lives and allowed us to accomplish more than ever?" In many ways, yes, it has! Yet, there are problems that come along with technology. If you will take a closer look at all of your devic-es you will realize the need to approach these modern conveniences with definite boundaries. Technology can be a friend or foe, so balance is everything.

To put it simply, we're distracted. The Encarta Dictionary provides the following two definitions of the word *distracted:*

1. Pre-occupied; showing a lack of concentration

2. Anxious; so worried or upset as to be unable to think clearly or act sensibly

Oh my goodness! We are constantly distracted! However, we don't consider ourselves distracted because we've chosen to put a spin on our behavior, describing it instead as "multi-tasking." Wikipedia.com defines human multi-tasking as, *the performance by an individual appearing to handle more than one task at the same time. The term is derived from computer multi-tasking. An example of multi-tasking is listening to the radio while typing an email. Some believe that multi-tasking can result in time wasted due to human context switching and apparently causing more errors due to insufficient attention.*

Other sources define multi-tasking as simply, the *simultaneous performance of more than one task.* Since when we try to do two things at once, we don't do either of them very well. I prefer Wikipedia's definition as the most honest and accurate.

Do you disagree? The fact that we are not capable of performing multiple tasks at high levels is something all parents have always known and not hesitated to say, "YOU CAN'T WATCH TV AND DO YOUR HOMEWORK AT THE SAME TIME."

They were right. It simply doesn't work. We can watch TV and then do a little homework, and then watch a little more TV and then do a little more homework; but we cannot perform two tasks of any complexity, *with excellence*, at the exact same time. If we try (and we all do), it is a fact that neither task is ever completed *to the best of our ability*.

For better or worse, technology is on the move, continuing to increase the potential for us to be distracted by newer, faster, fancier and more intricate, time-consuming gadgets. Take, for example, just a few things that I've seen people anxiously trying to do (multi-tasking) while driving: texting, dialing the phone, talking on the phone, emailing, looking up contacts, reprogramming a GPS, eating, surfing the radio, surfing the satellite radio, surfing the web, playing with their iPod and my all time favorite, putting on make-up. When I say, "Putting on make-up," I don't mean applying a little lipstick after lunch as you start the car! I actually witnessed a lady looking in her rearview mirror and applying her mascara as she flew by me literally doing 80 mph!

Every day I observe people engaged in meaningful conversations at the same time they are performing other activities, never giving their undivided attention to anything. Few people seem to have prolonged, technology free, face-to-face conversations. I've noticed that the younger generation prefers texting to talking. We have so many television channels that a lot of people tell me their DVR (digital video recorder) is full of shows they simply must catch up on. I've noticed that people become lost surfing the Internet and updating their various websites, often for hours on end.

I've also observed that people are always checking something. They check messages of all sorts, news reports, sports scores, the stock market, their friends' statuses and thanks to an onslaught of unbelievably advanced phone applications, they can check everything from home security cameras to traffic reports and restaurant ratings. Everyone seems to have to stay on top of "it" whatever "it" is.

The cost of staying on top of "it" is unfortunately keeping us from enjoying our lives and distracting us from God's voice as He desperately tries to get our attention. We're living life in a blur of activity and at the end of the day or sadly, it might be at the end of a person's life, we reflect back on it all with bitter regret and the gnawing feeling that we missed our purpose in life. Too often we see the fruit of this lifestyle in ruined health, poor family relationships, and things we've accomplished that are empty and vain.

We're missing out on real life because we were trapped in *The Big Gray Swirl.*

WHY A GRAY SWIRL?

I received the term *The Big Gray Swirl* from something I observed at one of my son's Cub Scout meetings. The kids were painting and I, being fully engaged in the moment, began to pay special notice to the way two of the boys were utilizing their colors. One actually reminded me of myself at that age and the way I might have painted a picture. He began by painting a big red spot in the center of his paper. Next, he painted a yellow spot directly over the red spot and, upon realizing that the two colors blended together to create orange, he continued to experiment further, adding a green spot to the orange spot and then blue and purple and so forth and so on until the entire artistic creation appeared to be one big gray swirl. He then took one look at his creation, the final result of all his efforts thus far, and did something remarkable, he threw it away. At that moment, I received the thought from God that that was how most people lived their lives. The other boy painted one corner red, another corner green, a square in the middle blue and so on. When he finished his painting it looked like a stained glass window. He looked at his creation, the final result of his efforts, and said, "Dad, can I hang this up when I get home?" Put this story in your pocket for now and we'll pull it out later.

Chapter 2

The Good the Bad and the Ugly of my Journey

Proverbs 16:9 "A person may plan his own journey, but the LORD directs his steps." (God's Word, translation)

I want to share my journey and struggle out of *The Big Gray Swirl*, so you can better understand how I've lived out the conclusions of this book and why the tools I will relate here will change your life.

The truth is I found myself chasing what I thought was the high life. During my early twenties I was living in New York City. I'd left behind my childhood faith and my experiences of God's faithfulness for life in the fast lane and my own piece of *The American Dream*.

I was in the restaurant business where I was a dining room manager and rubbed shoulders with the rich and famous. I was making a lot of money, partying among celebrities, and even though it was something I had pursued, when caught, it was disappointing. I don't know what magic I had hoped to find, but the thing that I had been striving for, that excitement, that fun, that life in the fast lane had given me a good sneak peek and there was nothing there for me. Sure, there was fancier food, more expensive alcohol, better entertainment, nicer clothes and whiter teeth, but I was still unfulfilled and empty.

So many times we think we're building a palace but once we live in it awhile we realize it's a prison.

I was living a selfish, over-indulgent, immoral life with little to no consideration for anyone else but myself for six years. I was miserable and ashamed at how I had taken for granted, used or mistreated so many good people, including myself.

Often I would sit up on the roof of my apartment building and find myself soul searching and remembering; one man in particular floated back to my recollection. He was the pastor of the small Lutheran church where I was confirmed. He lived in a little maroon house alongside that church. He referred to his little house as his parsonage. I marveled at the way this pastor lived his life. Considering the fact that his entire life revolved around his little maroon house, his little church, and serving his little congregation. I had been amazed at his constant state of happiness, contentment, and calmness. I mean, how could a man with very little money, living such a simple life be satisfied?

As an inquisitive boy I had asked him, "Don't you want more out of life?" The pastor had replied, "My life is rich, full and I have all I want." I remember thinking that was impossible; I mean *can anyone really* have everything they want? He had truly fascinated me. His contentment had puzzled me because like many of us, I didn't measure success by the simplicity of being who God made you to be.

Could it be that our trophies of success are too often measured through the eyes of the world?

Money. Beauty. Fame. While these are glamorous possessions in life, their unforgiving demands crush our contentment and peace if we strive for them. In each of us lies a need to communicate with God and realize our own eternal quest for a life whose meaning will never die, full of deeds that will never be forgotten.

This man's life was a bold statement in contrast to those who spent their days chasing things that would never matter in the end. He had everything he wanted because all he wanted was to accomplish God's purpose for his life.

After contemplating the lives of other people, I began thinking about my own life. The day I was born my grandmother told my parents I would be a preacher some day; at my confirmation it was repeated again. I had always been fascinated by men of God, especially my Lutheran Church pastor. What did my childhood pastor know that I didn't know? Was my grandmother right about what I should be doing?

FINDING FAITH

And so there it was; I had been ignoring God for six years. I was dry and I felt lost. I was simply disillusioned. There had been no magic. Then, one day I phoned a girl, I'll nickname Faith. I asked her to come visit me in New York City. Faith and I never dated but we had traveled together with a group called "Up with People" and we loved hanging out together. She agreed to come. I couldn't wait to see her because we were crazy together. We would be in New York City, and I was sure that I'd be able to ignore my emptiness with the distractions of food, drink, music, dancing, sporting events and sightseeing. When I picked Faith up, however, she surprised me by asking if I would take her to a church, specifically, a church on Fifty-first and Broadway. I told her that no such church existed because, in fact, my restaurant was also at that location and there wasn't a church there. She insisted, even calling the church by name, "The Church on Times Square." Well, sure enough, when we got to Fifty-first and Broadway, there was a little sign around the corner saying "The Church on Times Square" and I had never noticed it. It was a theater that at some point was converted into a church; David Wilkerson was the pastor. On that night, in that church, I rededicated my life to the Lord in a big way; God changed me. I could tell that I was a new person. That day God removed all of the darkness and *yuckiness* inside me.

After church, Faith gave me her Bible and a Keith Green record. We prayed together and talked about the Word of God. I committed to her that every morning I would listen to the Keith Green record, pray and read my Bible on the subway ride into work. I started walking with God again because God sent Faith. Later I found out that in addition to my mother, Faith and her roommate; several Christians I traveled with in "Up With People" had been praying for me, also.

I was awed by how faithful God was even when I wasn't. God hadn't been sitting around waiting for me to come back, He had been pursuing me.

During this time I started remembering how much I loved God and the ways He had been faithful in my childhood. Through every trial He had found some way to show me that He was faithful just like he was when I was in the fifth-grade.

BLACK PORCELAIN ANGELS

My grandmother didn't believe that evidence of God's faithfulness was found in the lack of storms one had, but rather in the number of storms one has weathered.

When I was in fifth-grade my family moved. I went from a well integrated school in one town to a school where I was the first and only African American in the fifth-grade.

There was one particular incident that always stood out in my mind. It was one that occurred during gym class while playing kick ball. That day, while standing in line to take turns at kicking the ball, a particular group of students, myself included, had become unusually rowdy and the teacher monitoring the line was quick to notice. Unsure of the instigators and in an attempt to quiet the ruckus, the teacher began pointing down the line, asking each student individually if they indeed were the culprit of all the horsing around. The response from each student, of course, was the same, a firm, "No", but she continued asking nonetheless. When she finally made it to my place in the line I looked up at her and replied, "No, I'm an angel." It was at that moment that a girl's voice from somewhere in the line commented rather matter-of-factly, "You can't be an angel. There's no such thing as black angels. I've never seen a black angel. You can't be an angel, because you're black." Her comment caught the attention of the line and soon everyone was offering an opinion, "Yeah, that's right, you can't be a black angel! There's no such thing! Have you ever seen a black angel? I've never seen a black angel! Yeah that's not possible!" This went on for only a few seconds before the teacher, who'd been listening to the entire exchange, yelled at everyone to knock it off and things finally fell silent.

On the way home from school, I thought about what the kids had said. I couldn't remember ever seeing a black angel either so I asked my mother if there *was* such a thing and, of course, explained where this was all coming from. My mother assured me that there are angels that look like every type of person God has ever made. So yes, of course there were black angels! She made sure to remind me *not* to let the other kids see that they were bothering me. In spite of what would happen she encouraged me to believe that God was faithful.

I didn't question my mother's admonitions at all. She had a history of reassuring me and being right. If I wanted to I could have thought of a hundred reasons why there was nothing ahead for me but gloom and doom. However, contrary to all logic or evidence, I believed my mom. Later in life I would transfer that trust in Mom to trust in God.

Mysteriously enough, a little black angel appeared in my house not long after that incident. It was a little porcelain angel that had obviously been re-painted to have brown skin and black hair. Although I knew that mom had painted it, I never thought for one minute that what she had said about black angels wasn't true.

I thought it was cool that even though other people didn't make black angels there was no reason why we couldn't make black angels. If reality didn't agree with the truth, Mom and Dad believed you could change the reality.

So God was faithful in my childhood. He was faithful later when I walked away from Him and in the next chapter of my life I would discover my purpose and begin to form the real premises of this book.

Pursuing Who God Made Me to Be

Faith called to tell me that the church she'd been attending was planning to start a bible school in the summer and that she felt I was meant to be a part of this. I talked to my pastor, my parents, my friends, and I prayed a lot trying to wrap my mind around the idea of stepping out of my life and going to bible school in Texas. I didn't want to go. I was a twenty-five year old living in a nice apartment on Roosevelt Island making good money. The move would kill my resume, I mean, where is there room for "took off to try a little bible school?" I'd be going to a place that I had never been or seen. I also didn't want to go to Texas simply because of the stereotypes. Once I heard a joke that went something like this, "What's the difference between a New York Zoo and a Texas Zoo?" The punch line is, "The animal enclosure of the New York Zoo will have the name of the animal in English, the scientific name in Latin, and a description of the animal's habitat. The Texas Zoo will have the name of the animal and a recipe of how to best cook it."

After some deeply personal dealings between God and myself, I finally decided to go to Texas. I gave away my bed, my couch, and everything I owned except for a suitcase, a hanging bag, a briefcase, and a walking stick that I had bought in Luxemburg. It was the greatest leap of faith I'd ever taken and a test to see if I really believed that God was faithful.

I didn't think I could be in "The City" one minute and a few hours later in Texas so I decided to take the bus to have a few days to transition. As I arrived at the Manhattan Port Authority, a uniformed man approached me and said he would take my bag for me. Before we got to the counter he asked for my ticket to see where I was going; then he asked for a few bucks to tip the guys who load the bus. In my malaise of leaving my life behind, I completely forgot all my street smarts and pulled out the wad of cash I had for my entire trip to Texas. I gave him a few dollars. The uniformed man checked in my bags but didn't give the man at the counter the money I gave him. I thought, "That was strange!" But what would have been a big red flag was just a curious observation on this day. The uniformed man gave me my ticket back and said "I'll show you where your gate is." As I followed him, hardly paying attention, I noticed there seemed to be fewer and fewer people around. Then for some reason, an enormous wave of fear washed over me and I absolutely knew I was about to be attacked. I turned around and saw two men walking quickly toward me. As I processed what was happening I started shouting, "I don't know them. I don't know these two guys. I don't know you. Who are you?" God blessed me with a really loud voice so everyone looked in our direction. As the two men ran off I realized that I had almost been mugged.

I went to my real gate and had a few minutes to wait. While I was standing by myself close to the gate, the man in the uniform approached me once again. He quickly showed me a knife and said, "Give me your money and you won't get hurt!" I saw a police officer in the distance and decided to shout, "This is the guy you're looking for!" The man walked off not knowing I had never really spoken to the officer.

I then thought, "Seriously God, I'm going to get killed in the bus station. I leave everything to get killed in the bus station. A little help would be nice, please?"

Finally, I got on a Greyhound bus and headed off to the great unknown. However, just outside the Port Authority our bus was shot at because there was a bus strike at the time and our driver was a scab. As I looked at the little bullet hole in the window in front of me, I thought again, "Wow! I survived living like a heathen just to almost get mugged, threatened with a knife and shot at!"

I thought, "Aren't things supposed to get easier now that I'm back following God?"

Soon the police came; we switched buses and made it out of town just fine. I had a lot of time on that trip to think about God. As I reflected on my life until that moment, something was being birthed in my spirit. I thought about the challenges in elementary school, my time in high school after my brother died, that dreaded decision to leave God when I was in college, the quiet prayers of "Up With People", believers who I didn't even know were praying, the righteous words of David Wilkerson, and my departure from New York. As I sat through that long bus ride, I didn't understand why everything had happened the way it did, however many small things happened along the way that convinced me, God was in control and was truly directing my steps.

You've got a choice to either end up with a sour attitude and bitter outlook on life or taste the sweetness that God provides even in the midst of the trials. You must recognize God's divine interactions, those brief and seemingly quiet communications that can protect you from being poisoned by fear and bitter foreboding. With a few skills to build your awareness, you can savor God's persistent presence. You can be equipped to recall and reflect on those divine interactions providing the sweet realization of His love and faithfulness.

REHAB, GOD? REALLY?

As I arrived in Texas, little did I realize that my life was about to really slow down and I was about to "detoxify" from the life I'd been living. Instead of taking a job and living in an apartment while going through bible college, God had other plans.

Within an hour after I arrived at the little church in Texas, the pastor I'd been making my arrangements with, before I moved from New York, pulled me aside and said he thought I was supposed to work in the church's men's drug and alcohol rehabilitation home in lieu of finding an off-campus job, as we had discussed. I was more than a little surprised, hesitant and unsure what the pay or living arrangements would be. Nonetheless, I thought I'd be a team player and agreed if it would help them. I was told the head of the men's home would fill me in on all the details.

I was taken directly to the men's home to meet with the head of the home. As I walked into his office he asked me if I was on any drugs. I answered, "No." He wrote it down on a form and started to ask many other personal questions. At some point I stopped him and asked, "What's the purpose of all the questions?" He replied that it was part of the intake process. I replied, "Intake…?" He then informed me that if I was going to work in the home I first needed to complete the 90-day drug and alcohol rehabilitation program. I would leave the home to go to bible school classes when the men left for work crew and come back to the home when classes were over. My job would be the house cook. One hour and a search of all my possessions later I was shown to my room. I walked in, met my roommate and was assigned my bunk.

PRAISE IN THE NIGHT

As I lay in bed unable to sleep and chatting with my roommate I was told we were allowed to quietly listen to one radio station at night. So I turned on the radio and heard, "This is *Praise In The Night*", which was a show that talked about God and played worship music all through the night. I laid there and heard a soothing voice talking about the wonders of knowing God. I heard beautiful music all about God and His kingdom. People would call in and talk about what God showed them or what they experienced. I may not be where I am today if it wasn't for *Praise In The Night*. Their stories were proof of God's involvement in the lives of His children and it grew my faith in God's ability to steer my course.

During this time I studied a lot, learned a lot, and went through a lot of healing. I hadn't realized the toll that the previous quarter century had taken on my life. It turned out that learning to stuff down large amounts of pain and suffering so I could go about my day was not good for me. In fact, it's not good for anyone although many of us do this. I don't blame anyone for encouraging this strategy; after all they were rubbing butter on burns back then, too.

Like so many of us I wanted to change without having to change too much. I wanted to change but stay in my comfort zone.

In retrospect, concerning my hectic life in New York, I realized I needed to CALM DOWN. If I set up the same hectic, 90 mile per hour life I had before and tried to just add God to it, I would have gained very little. Also, although God was faithful to take away most of my pain as it came, I still needed to learn how to be a whole person, one who was open, honest, transparent and fully engaged in the here and now.

Like everyone else, I faced my own set of trials that would either embitter me and steal my faith or set my life on the path God planned for me.

Slowing down taught me something; I actually had time to think. That led me to write down the things God showed me and put to paper the ways God helped me. It also proved His faithfulness to me. Through the benefit of hindsight, I realized if I had rushed into a full time job, bible school and started running in every direction again I would have missed out on those interactions with God. Like those who shared their stories on *Praise in the Night*, I realized I had my stories, too.

Later on I would realize how powerful this revelation of slowing down and savoring God's presence would be to so many others I would help on their journey of purpose and intimacy with God.

Chapter 3

Turn Off, Tune In, Hear God

Eventually I became a pastor. Along with my pastoral duties, I took on the role of president of the drug and alcohol rehabilitation home, president of the men's homeless shelter and founder of the county's first women and children's homeless shelter. Somehow, in the middle of everything, I even managed to get married and become a father. As I worked with the various people coming and going at the shelters and rehabs, I noticed that the vast majority of them were frantically busy searching for ways to change their circumstances. They were immersed in the cares of this life, acting as if their ideas and their way of thinking was their only hope. They struggled with their faith and were trapped inside a system of behavior and thinking that I would later call, *The Big Gray Swirl.*

Now, when I say that these people struggled with faith, I don't mean faith as in the existence of God or faith as in the fact that God loved them or that God was their father. Their struggles with faith concerned the question of whether or not God was faithful and whether or not He did, indeed, speak regularly into the everyday lives of His children. They struggled with the faith that allows a person to say from the deepest part of their being, "God is faithful in the midst of tragedy and difficult circumstances."

Regularly, people would say, in no uncertain terms, that God hadn't said anything or done anything for them in a long time. My response was to simply say, "That's not true. You have either not recognized or not remembered what God has said to you or showed you." This would amaze them and many would push me for answers as to how this could possibly be. "I don't know," I would reply. Then I would tell them that the Bible says, "The LORD is good. His mercy endures forever. His faithfulness endures throughout every generation. (Psalms 100:5)"

If our reality doesn't reflect the truth we need to change our reality.

I would ensure them that I could equip them to recognize, remember and respond to what God was saying to them. I began encouraging them to read their Bible and attend Bible studies or classes. I would encourage them to participate in prayer groups, establish a personal quiet time and basically get in relationship with a group of people who would love God and would love them.

Equally, I encouraged them to immediately write down anything they thought, saw or experienced that might be from God. This was not to be a journal entry of daily and weekly events but a real time activity that chronicled their interactions with God. To assist with this activity, I would offer coaching tips from time to time such as, "Look for the favor of God, perhaps in a favor from a person or in a situation that seems out of the ordinary. Listen for God talking to you as you go through your day, interacting with people, seeing things, doing things. Try to be extra sensitive to thoughts you have which may be thoughts that God is giving you."

GOD STARTED TALKING

As an example of chronicling our interactions with God, I would tell the following story. "While driving one day, I noticed a billboard containing a picture of a scantily clad woman and I instantly had a thought, 'True beauty is healthy spirit, soul, and body.' Now, I had never had that thought before and the thought itself felt a little different. Up until this point, I had always defined beauty as a pretty face and a nice body. I pulled into a parking lot wrote the words, 'True beauty is healthy spirit, soul, and body' on a piece of paper. Later, when I reminded myself of this new thought, I meditated on it. During my meditation, I received an even more refined and complete definition of beauty, 'A person who submits themselves to God and is in the process of allowing God to make them as healthy as they can be, spirit, soul and body'. Now that is a beautiful person. I concluded the thought was from God."

I wasn't asking for a new definition of beauty. I wasn't praying for a new definition of beauty. I didn't even know I needed a new definition of beauty. However, by being fully aware of the possibility that God may speak to me during my drive and by being tuned into God, He gave me a new definition anyway. More significantly, because I captured this thought in real time by writing it down, years later I can still remember what God said to me and have passed it along to my children.

We know from many studies over the years that the mere act of writing something down, gives us a much better chance of remembering it. Then if we re-read and meditate on what we've written, we will almost certainly incorporate it into our lives and pass it on to our children.

So I told people this story and then sent them out. Within a few weeks, some came back amazed and said, "As incredible as it is, you were right. I know now that God was faithful before but I just didn't receive it or I didn't remember it." However others would insist, "God wasn't talking to me before but once I started chronicling His faithfulness, boy, God started talking." Either way, both groups recognized that, Wow, God will show you things, talk to you, and be with you every day, all day.

How God Reunited
a Father and Daughter

As with all my stories, I give people nicknames to protect their privacy. So Big Mike had struggled with a drug problem for many years before he found himself at my homeless shelter. Having destroyed every family relationship he had, his life was in shambles. As Big Mike progressed through the program, I came to discover that the greatest desire of his heart was to re-establish a relationship with his 12 year-old daughter, Joy. He continually talked about the hurt, pain, and disappointment he had caused his daughter and how he felt that his relationship with her was beyond repair. He agonized over the fact that his daughter and her mother had stopped taking his calls a long time ago.

I came up with a plan for Mike and his daughter to find healing through God. Presenting Mike with 50 blank cards and envelopes one day, I challenged him to begin sending a note to his daughter each Thursday so that she would receive it on Friday when she came home from school. I explained that he should offer no apologies because, at this point, apologies from him would have no meaning. I told him that there were things a father should say to his daughter and that God, being her true Father, would give him the things to say in each card so that Joy's heart would be healed in the process.

When the first Thursday passed, I asked if he had sent a note, Mike replied that he had not and explained that God wasn't giving him anything to say. I stressed that I was certain God was speaking to him but that he, however, wasn't paying attention. He lamented that he prayed every morning, sitting still before God and still nothing would come to him. So I gave him a pocket sized notebook and explained that God was going to give him a message for Joy sometime in the next few days and that this message could come at any time. God may speak during the day as he drove around, or as he ate his lunch, or even as he combed his hair. For Big Mike, the challenge would be to immediately write down what God had to say or else he would risk forgetting the message soon after.

Almost immediately, Mike began receiving messages from God and writing to Joy. His messages to Joy were short and simple and went something like this:

"Joy, I have been praying for your friends all week. I hope everything is fine between you and your friends. I know a girl as sweet as you wouldn't have any problems making friends. I pray you have good friends. If a friend likes to make fun of other people but is nice to you, be careful because one day they will probably make fun of you, too. I hope you had a good week in school and a great weekend with your friends. If you ever want to talk, call this number and ask for me. I love you, Daddy."

Weeks and then months passed without a response from his daughter but Mike continued to send his note each Thursday. Having advanced to the point in the rehab program where he could begin to work, Mike started to add a little money to each card along with a note to Joy to do something nice for herself or for her mom. However, as time continued to pass, Mike confided to me that he was fairly certain they were tossing the notes into the trash before they were ever read. Even though I could see his unbelief, I encouraged him to keep going and to trust that things would be okay.

One day, the phone rang at my home. On the other end, a little girl's voice said, "Hi, my name is Joy. Can I talk to my Daddy?" I asked her to hold on and I ran as fast as I could over to the homeless shelter. I found Big Mike and told him that there was a little girl on the phone asking for her daddy. If I remember right, his reaction was, "What do you want me to do about it?" I laughed and said "No, it's Joy! It's Joy on the phone!" Mike jumped up off his seat, ran over to my house. He and his daughter talked for the first time in a long time. Big Mike and Joy continued to speak regularly on the phone. After awhile, Joy would come and stay with my daughter, my wife, and I. She and Mike would spend all day together. It was obvious to me that by providing Big Mike with the words he needed to write in each of those notes God had healed Joy's heart and shown Himself faithful to Big Mike.

Throughout my time as a pastor at this little church with the drug rehab and homeless shelters, I found myself constantly repeating the words, "God is faithful and He's talking to you and showing you things all the time. Let me equip you to recognize and remember them. At some point your children will also be blessed to have your stories and life-lessons."

Big Mike and the others didn't know how to turn off the busyness of the world, tune in to God's hand in their lives and hear God in the little messages He would send them through other people, situations or thoughts.

Something as simple as a new state of mind, a pocket sized spiral notebook and a golf pencil helped change their lives and those they loved.

FROM RAGS TO RICHES, EVERYONE STRUGGLES

After ten years, I moved on to become a staff pastor at a very affluent North Dallas church. This particular church had many wealthy members and I was amazed to see that they too struggled with faith in the same manner as those members of my previous church. Again, I speak not of struggles of faith relative to the existence of God or to the fact that God loves us and is our true father, but rather struggles with faith that God is indeed faithful and regularly speaks into our everyday lives.

Somewhere in life, I had inadvertently adopted a belief that those of us with more money had an easier time believing that God was faithful than those of us with less, little, or no money. Obviously, I was very wrong. I saw that trouble comes to the rich and poor and money doesn't fix much.

My observations during this period soon had me realizing that far too many of us walk through life pretending to believe, at least on the outside, that God is faithful all the time when deep down inside we are actually asking ourselves the question, "What has He done for me lately?"

With my grandmother's generation believing, "God is faithful" and my generation asking, "What has He done for me lately?" I began to wonder if my grandchildren would inherit a church of deism. A church where members, while believing that God created everything, that Jesus is the Son of God, and that God will receive those that have faith in Jesus Christ, ultimately do not believe that God really intervenes in the everyday affairs of His children. Simply put, deism is a belief that God, after creating the world and making the rules, basically sat back, leaving us to keep the rules and be as good as we can be until we die and go to heaven.

MY BIG POINT

People in the homeless shelter and the members of my North Dallas church found that God is present and active in their everyday lives. God wants to direct our steps daily. God has shown himself faithful to us more times and in more ways than any of us can imagine or remember. Our children should read of God's faithfulness in our lives because God is faithful today, yesterday and tomorrow.

When you feel the sting of prejudice, God is faithful. When your brother dies, God is faithful. When you get to travel the world with a group like, "Up With People", God is faithful. When you walk away from God, God is faithful. When you come back to God, God is faithful. When you forsake all you have to go some place you've never been, God is faithful. When you are addicted to drugs, God is faithful. When your little girl hates you, God is faithful. When your little girl comes back to you, God is faithful. And, when money can't change your problems, God is faithful.

I'M PERPLEXED

I knew all of this to be true and yet, I was perplexed. I simply could not understand what was happening in our lives that stopped so many of us from recognizing, remembering, drawing strength and faith from the clear and present evidence of God's faithfulness in our lives. It was clear to me that we all have many stories of God's faithfulness in our lives, whether we remember them or not and that we need those stories and our children need those stories.

So I started praying and looking for an answer to the question, "Why? Why weren't we recognizing, remembering and passing along our stories and life-lessons of God's faithfulness?"

THE WHEELS IN MY MIND STARTED TURNING

It was then I started to pay attention to how the technology revolution was affecting us. As these questions prevailed in my mind, it didn't take long before I realized how busy everyone is today. I was somewhat confident that this shift to a culture of busyness in an environment of distractions had to be related to our lack of faith in the faithfulness of God. We aren't taking the time to tune into God so He can direct our steps. We aren't looking for, recording or remembering God's faithfulness in our lives. Why?

When I asked people about their busyness the answer was pretty much the same. I was told, "I don't have enough time as it is. I can't slow down. I don't know why I don't have dozens of stories of God's faithfulness at the ready, but I know I don't have enough time as it is."

Why do we feel we never have enough time? My conviction is that God gives us plenty of time.

I believe if we would calm down a little, expecting God to constantly talk to us and capture what He said, we would grow in confidence, letting God direct our steps and grow in our faith.

So how do you change someone's perception of time? Why do so many people have a perception of time as flying by in a big blur, while others who are just as productive, seem to notice the beauty and nuances of life and perceive time so differently. We need to realize we can be highly productive without rushing around. We need to perceive the time we have differently. We all have time to fulfill God's purpose for our life.

As a pastor I felt the need to find a way to help people perceive time differently. So I prayed and started researching what factors affect our perception of time.

Chapter 4

Our Perception of Time

How confident are you that we recall segments of time accurately? If an event lasts a minute do we recall it as a minute? Do we recall an hour as an hour or a day as a day? You may be surprised but most of us in our culture today have a distorted recollection of time and the ramifications are significant.

The intensity of our awareness in a given experience affects our perception of time when recalling that experience.

AN EXPERIMENT

An experiment has been conducted several times using everyday people. Participants allowed themselves to be hooked to a harness that was then attached to a cable. The cable hoisted the harnessed person several stories up into the air above an enormous net or airbag. Without knowing exactly how high they were dangling each person would be released, plummet towards the earth and onto the airbag.

As soon as a person landed and was safely off the airbag, he or she was asked to picture with as much clarity and detail as possible exactly what had just happened. Recalling the experience in their mind, something interesting was discovered. In each case, the person's perception of how much time passed while they had been falling, was between one-third and two times longer than the actual time it took to reach the airbag.

The theory behind this result is that our brain works much like a video camera. A video camera records an experience at a speed of 30 frames, or pictures, per second. Upon playback, the images play at 30 frames, or pictures, per second, replaying the experience as it appeared in real time. So if you always take 30 pictures per second, of your child running 100 meters in

15 seconds, you would always end up with 450 pictures of each race. Now, if you had to miss your child's next race and your spouse went to take the pictures but came back with 900 pictures of the same 100 meter dash, it would be logical to assume your child ran a really slow race. However, if the truth was your spouse took 60 pictures per second, the race would have taken the exact same amount of time. Your initial perception of the experience being longer is due to a much larger amount of information captured in the same period of time.

An Epiphany

The belief is that our brain takes mental snapshots of what's going on throughout our day at a certain rate, whatever that rate may actually be. When we enter into a state of hyper-vigilance, like dangling high in the air, our brain begins "taking mental snapshots" at a faster rate. In others words, it's not that we are thinking faster or that time is moving slower but rather we are noticing every single little thing. We are taking mental snapshots of every nuance of the experience. Subsequently, when this experience is recalled, the massive amount of information present in our memories causes us to perceive the experience as lasting much longer than it actually did.

The intensity of our awareness in a given experience affects our perception of time when recalling that experience. Therefore it appears that a state of hyper-vigilance (or even giving our undivided attention) creates a perception of experiences lasting longer when we recall them.

This phenomenon is often experienced by police officers recalling life threatening incidents. Police officers will often describe these incidents as happening very fast while at the same time recalling the incident in almost slow motion. Intellectually, they may know that an entire incident lasted only a matter of seconds. However, because they were in a state of hyper-vigilance, they fully experienced every little detail of each microsecond of the incident, which upon recollection creates the perception of the event lasting longer than it did.

This phenomenon can also be experienced in situations other than life threatening incidents. Years ago, my parents invited myself and my family to join them on vacation in Cancun. Never before having stayed in such a luxurious resort, I saw things I had never seen before. This hotel featured pools with swim-up bars, glass bottom boats, jet skis, parasailing, and multitudes of people. There was something to do every single minute of every day of our stay. On the third day, I was sitting on the beach watching a pirate ship sail by (yeah I said pirate ship) and I felt as if I had been there an entire week! It was amazing to me, truly hard to believe, that it had only been three days. I had been so appreciative, thankful and fascinated by every moment of this experience that I had been "hyper-vigilant" reveling in every single moment of my day.

Our perception of time works in the opposite direction, also. If we are the opposite of hyper-vigilant there seems to be much less information gathered and a perception of that experience being very short. When we watch TV, we can actually use less of our brain than we do in REM sleep. Have you ever thought, "I'm just going to relax and watch some TV," only to find yourself surprised to discover that an entire afternoon or day had gone by? If you're like me you think, "Time never goes by this fast when I'm digging a ditch or listening to a boring lecture."

GOD ONLY USES OUR EXPERIENCES IF WE EXPERIENCE THEM

As a child, I lived in northern Indiana. In the summer my family would take a car trip to Nashville, Tennessee to visit my grandmother. Back then, about the only thing you could do to pass the time in a car was read a book. There weren't the DVDs and computers and MP3s we have today. Since my father preferred to leave late at night so we'd arrive first thing in the morning, we'd begin when it was dark and there was nothing for us kids to do. After hearing, "Are we there yet?" a few times, my father would say, "Just go to sleep and when you wake up, we'll be there. It's going to be fun." In anticipation of how fun it always was at Grandma's house I couldn't sleep. Sometimes I'd see long stretches of desolate road with headlights far in the distance and other times I'd see lights of some unknown city passing by. Sooner or later, of course, I'd get tired enough to fall asleep. I'd then wake up just as we pulled up to Grandma's house with Grandma standing on the porch. But I remember those trips as taking forever.

Currently I live in Texas, and now I take my children on a car trip to their grandparents' house. Only their trip takes about 18 hours! Like my father, I prefer to drive straight through the night to ensure we get there at an appropriate time in the morning. When the trip begins I announce, "The movie marathon has begun," and we fire up the DVD player. If the kids get tired of DVDs, we have little video and electronic game players they can occupy themselves with. Believe me, my kids love taking this trip, because I keep a multitude of distractions on hand to occupy their time.

My kid's perception of their trip to Grandma's house seems shorter to them than my trip to my grandma's house, even though their trip is more than twice as long as mine was.

All I had to do is stare out the window absorbing the fullness of a long trip and thinking about Grandma. My kids just spend some time zoning out in front of the TV and voilà, they're at Grandma's house.

God Redeems the Boredom of My Trips

At a very early age I developed a fairly unhealthy fear of death. This fear of death would cause me to have occasional panic attacks that would wake me up in the middle of the night. As a pastor whose job was to participate in funerals and to help others with this very same fear, I was understandably confused and disturbed by what was happening to me. Then one night, as I talked to God before a funeral, lamenting my frustration about my fear of death, He said this to me, "Alan, it's just like a trip to your grandma's house. As you drive through life sometimes it's a long, lonely road with just a couple of lights in the distance. Sometimes you're in a little town and sometimes you're in a big city. But at a certain point along the way, your Father is going to tell you it's okay. You can go to sleep now. You can trust me, when that time comes. And when you wake up again, it will be more incredible than you can possibly imagine."

God could use the experience I had as a child because I was fully engaged in experiencing it. It was very real to me so God could use it as a tool to heal me. For my kids however, God's ability to speak into their lives using their trips to their grandmother's house is lost because, to them, the trips virtually *do not exist in their memories.* That experience is one less experience they possess from their childhood and one less tool God can use. We need to take that trip with nothing but a few books. What I expect they will experience is:

Texas is big; Missouri has a lot of hills; in St. Louis there's a big arch called the Gateway to the West; Southern Illinois is really flat with lots of farmland; Chicago is really busy; Indiana is green and has a lot of cornfields.

They would, for the first time in their lives, really *experience* the trip. That experience would give God one more tool He could use to enrich their lives in some way.

Cute Stories but, What's Our Take Away?

If we are vigilant, fully engaged and undistracted in our experiences, our perception of time flying by when recalling our experiences will fade away. We will start to become free from the vicious cycle of feeling that our life is flying by in a big blur, making us feel that we have to do more rushing around and multi-tasking to redeem the time, which, means we are not fully engaged and hearing God in the midst of our experiences, which, makes us feel like we don't have enough time. Here are the cycles:

Negative Cycle

1. We don't feel we have enough time.

2. We feel we have to do more and we multi-task.

3. We are too distracted and busy to be fully engaged and vigilant in the midst of our experiences.

4. We are too distracted and busy to hear God in the midst of our experiences.

5. We don't feel we have enough time.

Positive Cycle

1. We have faith that God is faithful and we have enough time to do all we are called to do.

2. We are single-task minded and we do what we do with excellence.

3. We are fully engaged and vigilant throughout our day.

4. We are attentive to hearing God in the midst of our day allowing God to order our steps.

5. We have faith that God is faithful and we have enough time to do all we are called to do.

I grew up in a small town and trust me you didn't hear a lot of people commenting on how quickly Christmas came that year. With fewer distractions available and less of a culture of busyness, we spent a lot of time with each other breaking bread and talking. However, when we went bowling, that was all we were doing, bowling. When we went out to eat, that's all we were doing, eating out. When we went to the 4H fair, that's all we were doing, going to the fair.

I'm not saying that we can't have busy schedules, but the more you are able to be fully present in what you do while listening for God in the midst of the experience, the more you will realize that you have plenty of time for a full productive life.

Members of a mission trip I led to a small village in Mexico, regularly commented, "I don't want to return to the rat race. I feel so relaxed and so much closer to God." Although they had worked hard, been productive and accomplished a lot, it had not felt like it because they were fully engaged, hearing from God and I made them leave their distractions at home, their physical and mental distractions.

ONE MORE TIME SAINTS

Our perception of time affects our behavior and our behavior affects our perception of time.

The intensity of our awareness in a given experience affects our perception of time when recalling that experience.

Be fully present in what you do while listening for God in the midst of the experience.

Realize you have time to be and do all that God has created you to be and do. I'm not advocating complacency however an anxious, hectic lifestyle can be just as fruitless as a complacent one.

A Few New Questions

As I educated myself on how we perceive time and the effects of that perception on our behavior, I read a lot about how memory works. Although I felt I had tools for helping others to fully experience their day, hear from God, realize they have time and calm down, I wondered if we would remember what we've seen and heard from God in our experiences? Was there a component of how our memories work that was adding to our widespread lack of faith in the awesome faithfulness of God?

There were several articles I read which said it was not unusual for people to forget a great deal of information they once considered invaluable. How could this be? Was it really possible that God was very faithful to talk to us constantly but the problem was our memory?

Next, let's investigate how a culture of busyness and distractions affect our ability to remember what we've seen, heard, or experienced with God.

Chapter 4 Footnotes

For those who would like to engage in their own research, below are a few of the many articles I found helpful.

Stanford Encyclopedia Of Philosophy
"The Experience and Perception of Time"
First published Mon Aug 28, 2000; substantive revision Tue Nov 17, 2009
http://plato.stanford.edu/entries/time-experience/

Live Science
"Why Time Seems to Slow Down in Emergencies"
Charles Q. Choi December 11th, 2007
http://www.livescience.com/2117-time-slow-emergencies.html

Discovery Channel
"Time Warp" TV Series
In addition to the series, below is a link to a fun concentration game. My record is 00:49 seconds and 24 moves.
http://dsc.discovery.com/tv/time-warp/games/match/match.html

Chapter 5

How Our Memory Works

Did you know God designed our brains to constantly filter out irrelevant observations and experiences? Did you know, our brains are constantly deciphering our observations and experiences and deciding if to discard them or not? Is it possible, that when God whispers a thought into our ear, most of us will discard that thought by the end of the day?

Being able to retain the thoughts God gives us throughout the day will greatly impact all areas of our lives.

Our short term memory works much like the cache of a computer. Like a cache, our short term memory can only hold so many items before older items get replaced by newer items. Everyone seems to agree that the average adult should be able to hold at least seven items in their short term memory before the items are replaced, mixed-up, or forgotten.

The following simple test using random numbers demonstrates the capacity of your short term memory. Ask someone to give you one random single digit number, wait two seconds, and then write the number down; next, have them give you two random single digit numbers, wait two seconds, then write them down. The process continues with three random numbers, then four random numbers and so on. The average adult can remember seven numbers before he or she begins to forget or mix-up numbers.

Our long term memory is like the hard drive of a computer. If something is truly encoded in our long term memory, we can recall it without being prompted. The more often we access an item in our long term memory, the deeper it seems to be encoded and, therefore, the easier it seems to be remembered. Now, there are some idiosyncrasies relative to memory. It seems that you can have memories lightly encoded in your long term memory but not "indexed". This means that you have to be prompted to recall these memories or they will eventually fade away forever. True long term memories can be recalled without prompting. Some researchers think that most events are lightly encoded in our long term memory but not indexed, before they fade from our short term memory. The key is time, reflection and prompting.

TIME AND REFLECTION

Your brain needs time to reflect on an event in order to accurately decide if it is important. The more events that you experience and the faster that you experience them, the easier it is for your brain to inaccurately decide that something isn't important when, in reality, the event is one that should truly be remembered.

It is possible for something to happen of such immediate importance and intensity that our brain immediately encodes it to our long term memory. For example, if you happened to be standing in line at a bank as it was being robbed, you would instantly remember this no matter how many other experiences you had following the robbery. However, for normal, much less dramatic, events our brain needs time and reflection to decide whether or not to encode the experience into our long term memory. Generally, the minimum amount of time needed for our brain to process a conversation is 30 seconds. This means that if you give yourself just 30 seconds of distraction-free time to reflect on a conversation, your brain will be able to make much better decisions, not to mention that you also allow God time to comment on the conversation as well!

On the other hand, if you turn around and check your email, return a phone call, (where you're given two or three things to remember), start the car and turn on the radio, you probably will not remember the experience or conversation unless your brain lightly encoded it in your long term memory, which still means that you will not be able to recall the information unless prompted, because lightly encoded memories are not indexed.

PROMPTED MEMORIES

An example of a lightly encoded memory that would become lost forever unless prompted might entail you and I walking into church as I'm commenting to you about the pint of chocolate milk I had at breakfast. We get inside the church, talk to a few people, and then listen to the sermon. Later, as you are watching the evening ncws, a rcport comes on stating a nationwide recall on chocolate milk. The report states many have become very ill. This prompts you to think, "Oh no, Alan told me that he drank a pint of chocolate milk this morning!" This is an example of a prompted memory. Without the prompting of the news report, you probably would never have remembered the comment from that morning.

GOOD, BETTER AND BEST PRACTICES

A good way to ensure an experience becomes encoded into your long term memory is to immediately chronicle it. Anytime we write down an experience we tell our minds, "This is important!" A better way is to immediately chronicle an event and then shortly afterwards speak about the event. Speaking about an event reinforces what you chronicle because it additionally involves listening to yourself as you speak. However, the best way to ensure long term memory encoding is repetition. If we chronicle an experience, speak about the experience, and then revisit the experience for further reflection, the experience will be encoded in our long term memory and we will be able to recall it at will.

AGAIN WITH THE DISTRACTIONS

Another element that affects our ability to remember an experience is distractions. It took me a long time to realize that I could either videotape my children's events or I could actually see and enjoy my children's events. There were many times that I'd videotape my children's events only to have no recollection of the concert or sports game later when a certain moment from the experience would be mentioned in family conversations. However, if someone played the videotape, I would recall videotaping the event. Literally, I could recall the video shot and how I managed to zoom in at a perfect moment. But at the time of the event I wasn't really there, fully engaged, because I was too distracted with the process of videotaping. Now my wife and I take turns videotaping so there is always one of us fully-engaged and enjoying the moment. When I get to fully enjoy the experience of my children's events, I tell myself, "I want to remember this forever. I am fully present and engaged in this experience."

You simply cannot remember that which you did not experience.

Examples of distractions affecting memory occur all the time in the workplace. I do consulting work for churches and individuals. During one period, I was consulting with an individual who believed that God had called him to be a public speaker. After attending a couple of his events, I called a meeting and we sat for a critique of his public speaking. During the meeting I said, "When I was in high school,

Itzhak Perlman came to speak and I heard him say, 'Amateurs practice until they get it and professionals practice until they can't miss it!' " Now, the gentleman I was consulting, happened to be texting at the time I said this. He looked up at me and said, "Wow! That was really good. That's good." I responded, "Well, yes, I feel it's all about preparation."

As I was driving home after the meeting, I received a call from the client I just met with. He explained that he was driving home with his wife, trying to remember the quote I had shared with him. I proceeded to repeat the quote by Itzhak Perlman.

"Amateurs practice until they get it and professionals practice until they can't miss it."
—*Itzhak Perlman*

He responded before hanging up, "Yeah, that's it, that's it! Great! Thanks!" Now here's what I know that he didn't. If, while he's driving and doing other things, he simply allowed that quote to go into his short term memory long enough to repeat it to his wife, the chances are that he'd never remember it again. That gentleman could find himself feeling totally unsupported by God in his call of public speaking. Most importantly, he'd never remember God speaking through Itzhak Perlman's quote, giving him one of the biggest keys to an excellent presentation of any kind… preparation, preparation, preparation!

WHAT ARE WE TO CONCLUDE?

Research supports that memory is affected by our busyness and distractions during an experience. So it now seems highly likely that God has spoken to most of us at some point in the past and, although we probably said "That's really good," when we heard it, we quickly moved on and forgot it.

Too many of us are going through life from revelation to revelation forgetting each one along the way. This should not be.

A Theory is Born

Relying on my faith in the faithfulness of God, my journey to a Texas bible school, observations of our current culture, research into our perception of time and how our memory works, I developed a theory on what I came to call, *The Big Gray Swirl.* This is something I believe most of us are caught up in and are totally unaware.

CHAPTER 5 FOOTNOTES

For those who would like to engage in their own research, below are a few of the many articles I found helpful.

Intelegen Inc.
"Human Memory"
http://www.web-us.com/memory/human_memory.htm

Factoidz
"How Memory Works and Why We Forget Certain Things and Not Others"
http://factoidz.com/how-memory-works-and-why-we-forget-certain-things-and-not-others/

Lifehack
"Writing and Remembering: Why We Remember What We Write"
http://www.lifehack.org/articles/productivity/writing-and-remembering-why-we-remember-what-we-write.html

Scienceray
"Why Do You Forget Some Things and
Remember Others? Improve Your Memory"
http://scienceray.com/biology/human-biology/
why-do-you-forget-some-things-and-remember-
others-improve-your-memory/#5min

Chapter 6

What is The Big Gray Swirl?

*T*he *Big Gray Swirl* is a culture of busyness in an environment of distractions which distorts our perception of time and prevents us from fully recognizing or remembering the words, experiences, and directions from God. The result is weakened faith and very few, if any, stories of God's faithfulness recorded and ready to pass along to our children and grandchildren.

Those caught up in The Big Gray Swirl feel like they never have enough time because one activity runs into another and one day runs into another and life feels like one big blur.

Time seems to be moving so fast that they feel they have to try even more to redeem the time. With so much to do and so little time, they then rely on technology to help them multi-task and get more accomplished. By trying to do it all, they miss out on a rich life spent hearing and receiving from God while trusting in Him and following His directions.

EACH ACTIVITY IS ITS UNIQUE COLOR TO BE ENJOYED

Remember the Cub Scout meeting in the beginning of this book and how the boys were painting? One boy painted his colors on top of each other, creating a big gray swirl and the other boy kept his colors separated. In life, eating is a color. Meaningful conversation is a color. Checking our email is a color. Driving is a color. Working is a color. Taking a walk is a color. Reading a book is a color.

If we separate the colors of life and allow ourselves to become fully engaged in each activity, we can absorb all that experience has to offer and give ourselves the opportunity to hear God in the midst.

DON'T MOVE ON TOO FAST

Our propensity to forget what God shows us can be related to moving on too fast after God has interacted with us. After that Cub Scout meeting, I intentionally did not turn on the radio or touch my phone on the way home. I was determined to spend those five short minutes thinking about what I had experienced and heard. When I got home I wrote a few sentences about it. After that, I checked my phone messages.

Remember the average adult can only hold about seven items in their short term memory before something is lost. So what God showed me was one item. The scout leader giving us the next meeting date was two items. Driving home was three items. Listening to the baseball game on the radio would have been four items. Checking my phone for emails would have been five items. Answering my emails would have been six items. Calling home to see if my wife needed me to pick up anything on my way home would have been seven items. Remembering what to pick up while at the store would have been eight items. Checking my text messages would have been nine. Answering them would have been 10 and by then what God showed me would be long gone in less than five minutes.

Instead, I got home, took 60 seconds to write what I heard and a concept was born. Then, I checked all my messages and ran back out to get an item from the store.

So that one hour Cub Scout meeting was transformed from one more thing to do in my busy day, (while messing with my phone the whole time), to a life-changing experience from God that now gives texture and meaning to my life. I learned, from simply watching a young boy mix his paint colors that it is important to keep the colors of my life separate, thus keeping me free from becoming caught up in *The Big Gray Swirl*.

It cost me a couple minutes of time but I purchased a life-changing word from God with that time. God is faithful and life is exciting.

"MULTI-TASKING" IN THE BIBLE?
A Lesson from Jesus

The Big Gray Swirl has been around for a long, long time. Back when *The Big Gray Swirl* was an F0 tornado rather than the F5 it is today, people were still getting caught up in it. In the Bible, Luke 10:38-42 MKJV, we see a very busy and distracted Martha. The Bible reads,

> "And as they went, it happened that He entered into a certain village and a certain woman named Martha received Him into her house. And she had a sister called Mary who also sat at Jesus' feet and heard His word. But Martha was distracted with much serving and she came to Him and said, 'Lord, do you not care that my sister has left me to serve alone? Therefore, tell her to help me.' Jesus answered and said to her, 'Martha, Martha, you are anxious and troubled about many things but one thing is needful and Mary has chosen that good part which shall not be taken away from her.' "

In Martha's day, it was customary to bring your guests something to eat and drink. If Martha had nothing to serve, she would have simply sat down beside Mary. Apparently, they had food, plates and other things that the technology of the day afforded them and Martha was anxiously multi-tasking. She was hosting Jesus Christ, while running around and serving everyone, because serving everyone was what her culture said she should do. She was caught up in *The Big Gray Swirl*. Martha even became offended that Mary wasn't rushing around as well, to which Jesus said, *"Martha, you're anxious and troubled about many things but one thing is needful and Mary has chosen that good part which shall not be taken away from her."*

Mary recognized it was time to forget about everything else for a bit and fully be in the moment with Jesus. Because she did, she will remember it forever. Jesus said, *". . . Mary has chosen that good part which shall not be taken away from her."*

If Jesus would have come during Martha's quiet time when she was calm and prepared to receive from Him, there would have been no busyness. As it happened, however, Jesus came to spend time with her in the midst of her busy day. Today, we are busier than ever before and Jesus is still coming in the midst of our, busy fast-paced culture, to spend time with us.

It's a Cultural Thing

Our culture's definition of what it means to provide our children a good childhood gets many of us caught up in *The Big Gray Swirl*. Included in our culture are all the clubs, playgroups, music lessons, karate lessons, sports and activities, not to mention the obligatory trek to Disneyland which everyone knows is a child's rite of passage.

At what point did scheduling every spare minute with activities become healthy?

Since the time of Jesus, various believers have recognized the affect of culture on faith. Monasteries were created, in part, with cultural simplicity in mind so the residents could maintain their focus on God. I grew up in northern Indiana amongst the Amish, a community of people who value and maintain cultural simplicity and focus on God.

Am I saying we should pack up our cell phones, MP3 players, TV's, all other electronic technologies and head for the Amish life? *No, absolutely not!* Technology in and of itself is not a problem. I think it is possible to live in our current culture, utilizing technology, without getting caught up in *The Big Gray Swirl*. I will discuss this in much greater detail later. I think we can agree that as long as we live in this world, busyness will always be a temptation. Or as Jesus said, *"You are anxious and troubled about many things..."*

THE RAMPING-UP OF LIFE'S DISTRACTIONS

If you will recall, *The Big Gray Swirl* is a culture of busyness in an environment of distractions which distorts our perception of time and prevents us from fully recognizing or remembering the words, experiences, and directions of God.

The result is weakened faith and very few, if any, stories of God's faithfulness recorded and ready to pass along to our children and grandchildren.

Let's take a look at the increase in potential distractions that has taken place over the last fifty years. I was born in 1963. The babies born in the 60's were the last generation of children born before the sudden ramp up in technological achievements. Those of us born in the first half the 60's were most likely born into a household with only one phone, one TV, a radio or two, and a record player. That was it. Then, technology started ramping up.

In 1960, the average number of televisions per household was one. By the end of the 80's, the average home had two televisions and, by 2010, the average home had three. The 8-track tape cartridge came along in the mid-60's allowing us to play more than just the radio while driving and by default it gave us something else to fuss over. I remember that we carried a suitcase-sized tape case in our car for all our music.

Cable TV came along in the 70's and, at the same time, the VCR became a mass-marketed consumer product. Pong, the video game, was first released in 1972 with the home version of Pong following close behind in 1975. Home answering machines, pagers, and beepers came on the scene during the mid to late 70's. MTV launched, as did HBO, in 1981 with 24/7 broadcasting. Home computers became increasingly common during the 1980's. The mid-80's brought the popularity of video camcorders and family videotaping into the home. Next in line came my all time favorite, the first hand-held phone. This invention was first demonstrated by Martin Cooper in 1973 using a hand-set weighing just over four pounds. By 1990, 12.4 million people worldwide had cellular subscriptions. By the end of 2009, only 20 years later, the number of cellular subscriptions worldwide reached approximately 4.6 billion. That's 370 times the 1990 number!

CALL IT WHAT YOU WILL

I am choosing to call our culture of busyness, our distractions, our feelings of not having enough time, our lack of recognizing or remembering God in the midst of our day, *The Big Gray Swirl*. However, regardless of how someone might characterize these issues, it is problematic at best and a serious hindrance to increasing our faith and receiving direction from God at worst.

So how do we escape The Big Gray Swirl?

Chapter 7

Escaping The Big Gray Swirl

In our crazy 21st century world, is it possible to avoid getting caught up in a culture of busyness and distractions? The answer is a resounding, "Yes!"

We need to do three simple things:

First we need to trust that God, who is sovereign, will give us a fulfilling life and will direct our steps. God will give us as much time as we need to do what He specifically and individually created us to do.

Second, we need to separate the colors in our lives by doing one thing at a time with excellence, fully-engaged in the here and now.

Third, we need to be predetermined to chronicle, in real-time, whatever we think we are hearing or seeing from God and adopt a methodology to do it. Don't panic! It won't be painful.

If we do these three simple things, we will begin to see, feel, and hear God in the midst of our busy everyday lives. We will do what we do with excellence and remember it. Our faith will grow stronger. We will be able to allow God to direct our steps greater than ever before.

Slowly but surely we will no longer have any doubt that God does indeed love us, and walk with us, every day, through all circumstances. Lastly, but maybe most importantly, we will have a myriad of stories to pass along to the next generation giving them a head start in their journey of faith.

God Can Redeem Our Time

Most of us can intellectually accept that God is in control, but we act like it's all up to us. We act as if we have to stay on top of every little thing in our life or opportunities will be lost forever.

I am here to happily tell you this simply isn't true! Why? Because God is the redeemer! By separating the colors in our life and inviting God into the midst of our day, we allow ourselves to hear God, and thus receive from Him as He directs our steps. At this point something amazing takes place.

God will redeem our time and give us more opportunity than we could possibly create through our own effort.

Whether it is opportunity for our children or our business, God will redeem the time when you invite Him into the conversation. Just remember, checking our messages is a color. Conversations are a color. Eating lunch is a color. Spending time with our family is a color. Sitting in a prayer meeting is a color.

LITTLE CHILDREN ARE IMMUNE

Little children are always in the here and now and they absorb everything. If we could more like children, our speed of life could actually be quite fast without being stuck in *The Big*

Gray Swirl. However, we need to do what we do strategically and not try to do everything at the same time.

Busyness, distractions, and technology will work night and day to keep us stuck in *The Big Gray Swirl*. Plus, we put a lot of pressure on ourselves.

We don't ask ourselves, "What are we doing and why are we doing it?" nearly enough. Imagine God talking to us much like we talk to our children. Might God say, "Just because everyone else is rushing around, doesn't mean you have to?"

Does rushing around really save that much time anyway?

RELAX

Do you realize the difference between driving 20 miles across town at 60 mph and driving the same distance at 80 mph, risking your life, other lives, speeding tickets and stressing yourself out like a crazy person, is only, five minutes? That's right, you arrive five minutes earlier but you really lose fifteen minutes. Yes, you may get to your destination five minutes earlier but the fifteen minute drive is one big blur. You won't remember anything about it and that time is lost forever. Sixteen waking hours now becomes, by your perception, 15 hours and 45 minutes. This adds to your anxiousness of never having enough time. As a result, you drive faster the next time. And so the vicious cycle continues, over and over and over. It's time to relax!

If you relax and take the entire twenty minute drive to enjoy the city, talk to God, meditate on a conversation, listen to soothing music, or just take some nice deep breaths, you not only escape *The Big Gray Swirl*, but you give yourself the opportunity to hear from God. Maybe you'll realize that your son or daughter doesn't really need the activity you are driving them to (do they even really like going?). Perhaps you'll get a sense of peace about a business proposition. Maybe God will give you a new business idea as you drive.

I've discovered some of my favorite places to patronize while relaxing and driving from one part of the city to another. Look around as you drive and you will discover new things along old routes. You may find that God wants to redefine your definition of beauty as you drive. Remember my experience? Invite God into the conversation.

What Are We Doing and Why Are We Doing It?

Changing simple habits and behaviors is a good place to start. For example, I very rarely use restaurant valet parking. I enjoy the nice walk back to the car, savoring the experience of the meal. What are we doing and why are we doing it? Since I escaped the busyness of *The Big Gray Swirl*, life has become amazing. I used to walk in the park with my phone and MP3 player. I'd return personal calls and then listen to my MP3 player. Although I still listen to my MP3 player from time to time, mostly I just walk and enjoy God's creation.

Birds, Gnats & Dragonflies

One day not long ago, I was running through the park, the same park that I'd been running in for years, and I ran right into a cloud of gnats. I moved quickly to get away from this cloud and continued along the path. A little further down, I ran into another cloud of gnats. In fact, on that day there seemed to be several clouds of gnats positioned along my path, just hovering there for someone to run through them. As I was fully engaged and as hyper-vigilant as I could be in that experience, I began to notice that, with each cloud of gnats, there were also several dragonflies darting back and forth through the clouds. As I drew close, the dragonflies would buzz away but the cloud would remain.

I continued my laps around the park fascinated by what I was seeing. I wondered whether or not the dragonflies may have been eating the gnats. Just as quickly as I mentally asked the question, I felt I knew from God the answer was, "Yes!" From this answer, my thoughts turned to a verse from the Bible that states, "He feeds the birds of the air, how much more does He care for us?" I then shifted my focus back to my surroundings and became instantly aware of the birds that were everywhere, sitting on the phone wires, flying from tree to tree, pecking at the grass, and I realized that basic foundational beliefs were being reinforced through this experience.

When I arrived home, I immediately got on the Internet and searched for the word dragonfly with the confidence that it was God who told me they were eating the gnats. Amazingly, the first piece of information I found was a blurb stating how the dragonfly, being of a carnivorous nature, often feeds on other insects, most specifically gnats. I sat at my desk and meditated on this for a moment and then I wrote down the experience.

With every experience, no matter how seemingly insignificant, there is an aspect of God to be appreciated.

I decided to pay special attention to birds whenever I happened to be outside. In looking for the birds, I soon came to realize that there are more birds in the world than I could imagine! I don't think I've been outside for more than 30 seconds, looking for birds without seeing one. Honestly, how does God feed all those birds? There are birds everywhere. The birds that visit the bird feeder in my backyard, such a small number compared to the whole world, will go through a sack of bird seed every two or three days. I certainly don't know where the phrase, "You eat like a bird," came from because birds can eat! How much more will God care for me and feed me in every way I need?

GOD REALLY, REALLY LOVES ME!

What could I have possibly learned, or spiritually gained, from something as seemingly trivial as the fact that dragonflies eat gnats and, yes, that birds are everywhere? Well, from the moment of my experience at the park and from all my observations that followed everything kept pointing back to that simple Bible verse,

"Look at the crows: they don't plant seeds or gather a harvest; they don't have storage rooms or barns; God feeds them! You are worth so much more than birds!" (Luke 12:24 Good News Bible, translation)

God changed this little verse from an intellectual reality to an emotionally heartfelt reality. In a practical and real way I was given a greater sense of security of how much God loves us, how much God provides for us, and how God walks with us each and every day…all day. I mean, look how He provides for such a little creature as a bird. It only makes sense that, of course, He provides for us in much, much bigger ways! God loves us!

To this day, I notice little feathers on the ground, little feathers in the park, little feathers everywhere I go. It's become a running thing between God and I - noticing the birds. I smile and say, "I know you love me God, and you are providing for all of my needs."

BE STRONG, BE COUNTER-CULTURAL

In order to escape The Big Gray Swirl, *you must be strong enough to be counter-cultural.*

This means that you must push forward, be diligent, and even risk feeling momentarily uncomfortable as you chip away at all the multi-tasking.

For example, at a business meeting recently, I found myself attempting to have a conversation with a fifty-two year old man who insisted on texting simultaneously while we conversed. Finally I stopped talking. Annoyed, he looked up and said, "Go on." "No, that's okay" I replied, "I'll wait until you're done." "No, go ahead," he insisted. "No, really," I again replied, "I will wait until you finish texting and then we'll talk." In a very frustrated manner, he stopped text messaging, put his phone into his pocket, and growled, "Okay, fine." I looked at him and said, "We know when someone is driving and text messaging they're driving worse than the average drunk driver. So when I'm talking to someone and they're texting, does that mean I can expect the same type of retention and follow through as if I'm talking to a drunk person?" The man gave me a confused look and then said, "Fine, you have my attention!" and we proceeded to have our conversation.

The New ——— is Out!

Why do so many of us continue to line up outside of electronic stores for hours to be the first to get the newest gadget? We have become programmed to think that we need all this new stuff. Take, for example, the microwave. The microwave was billed as a timesaver, and it was. But, time for what? What, exactly, was it saving time for? Was spending time in the kitchen a waste of time before we could just "nuke" our leftovers? Did we make a conscious effort to decide how best to utilize this new technology? In blind faith, we simply accept the given assumption that any gadget that "saves time" or "makes our life easier" must therefore, be good.

We should ask ourselves if it's good or God, because many times good is the enemy of God.

We will go to almost any length to acquire a gadget whether we need it or not. Although, of course, we must need it if it indeed, "saves time" or "makes our life easier."

INCORPORATING NEW TECHNOLOGY IN OUR LIVES

Technology is dictating how we live our lives instead of us using technology with deliberate intention to enhance our lives. Understand that I certainly do not find everyday, common technology to be a problem in and of itself. The issue is how we incorporate new technology into our lives. Clearly, choices that stray from the norm, and in effect are counter-cultural, are often difficult ones to make because of peer pressure and other people's expectations. However, we need to define our way of life and how technology fits into it rather than letting the culture of the world define our lives and how technology fits into it. If technology interferes with the quality of our lives, we need to limit it, not be in fear of it.

Think about the cell phone. The cell phone was billed to save time, free us up, and make us safer. While the benefits of cell phones are fantastic, we've allowed plenty of room for our cell phones to diminish our life's experiences. Years ago, in New York City, it was my job to create the weekly shift schedule for the wait staff at a restaurant. On some weekends, this task was particularly difficult since we often found it hard to judge exactly the number of servers needed. As a result, we got into the habit of making out a list that basically scheduled staff members according to one of three shift categories: off, on, or "by the phone". Employees scheduled to be "by the phone" would then have to provide a phone number where they could be reached during that shift in the event that we needed them. One day, a union official stopped by and informed us that our "by the phone" scheduling was, in fact, illegal. We could not, under any circumstance, require an employee to be "by the phone" without compensating them. I suspect one of the wait staff, and rightly so, contacted the union official to question the fact that on some Saturday nights it was mandatory to be "by the phone", unpaid, on the slim chance that he or she would be called to work.

What makes this story particularly note-worthy is the fact that what was once illegal in the workplace is now commonplace due to the existence of cell phones. Technology makes it possible to stay in touch with the workplace no matter where we are. It has come to be expected that we'll stay in touch and be always "by the phone." This expectation has become so common that many employers will actually become upset if you don't answer an email, text or cell phone on your day off.

Now that I am free, I only take personal calls during my personal time and I rarely take business calls on my personal time. In the case of a true work emergency, I instruct people to text me the details of the emergency and I will decide when and how to respond.

Also, it is perfectly okay to schedule a time to check your messages. Earlier this year, I reached a phone that offered this as a voice message, "I'm sorry I missed your call. I return my messages at 10:00am and 2:00pm every day. Please leave me a message and I will return your call when I check my messages." When I heard that message, I thought, "Another person free from *The Big Gray Swirl*. Good for them!"

God's Daily Blessings

So as we become aware of the many ways in which *The Big Gray Swirl* is working to stop us from being fully present in our experiences, our next question is, "Can we stop *The Big Gray Swirl* from robbing our memory of our blessings, victories and revelations from God?" The answer is, "Yes!" Before discussing how to keep the memories of our experiences let's make sure we firmly understand how we are losing them.

Sometimes, when I'm sitting in a drive-through and I can see that the car behind me has only one person in it, I will say to the person at the window, "I am paying for myself and for the car behind me." In addition, I ask the person at the window to tell the person in the vehicle that I said, "This is a blessing from God." And with that, I'm given a funny look, my food, and off I go! I call it a "random act of kindness." It's just a small blessing, from God, in the midst of that person's day.

Unfortunately, the fact is, most of us wouldn't remember this blessing. Why? The answer is, once again, directly related to behaviors typical of those living in *The Big Gray Swirl*. They might pull up to the drive-through window receive their food and say, "You haven't taken my money." In response, the uncomfortable clerk might reply, "Well, the guy in front of you paid for you and he told me to tell you it was a blessing from God." The average person, always in a hurry, would probably respond with, "Great!" and pull away, more concerned about checking text messages, making a phone call, sending an email, and so forth. These tasks, by the way, are all executed while driving and eating so that any time saved on the ride back to work can be spent updating their Facebook status before the lunch break is over or the next meeting starts or the next appointment arrives.

Now imagine if you, as a receiver of God's drive-through blessing, would simply pull over into a parking space and take just one-minute to chronicle what had just happened. You would quickly have a new, inspiring, and permanent story to add to your faith bank! You would have a story to pass along to your children and grandchildren. The "cost" of adding this to your faith bank forever, is about one minute - just one minute.

Our Faith Banks

I refer to our collection of stories, illustrating God's faithfulness, as our *faith bank*. We need a tool by which we can quickly and simply chronicle and save our God moments, "on the fly", in the midst of our busy day, so that we can prompt our memories later and elaborate on the experience. I will share my vision on how existing technology can create a tool for this in Appendix C.

But first, do you realize the most popular social media sites are training us, especially our young people, to acknowledge an experience and forget it? I read this status from a friend the other day,

"Thanking God for guiding me safely off the freeway in the rain when my tire blew out on my way to work this morning. And, a big thanks to Aaron from Christ For the Nations for stopping and changing my tire for me. It was going to take over an hour for AAA auto club to arrive."

Now, if my friend got to work, wrote that status on their page and moved on with their busy day, they will most likely not remember the details of that blessing from God, through Aaron, years later. They certainly would not have the story in their faith bank, ready to pass along to their children.

Can little stories like the one above really build unwavering faith? I believe that the answer is, "Yes." Imagine a bookshelf with a book from your father, a book from your mother, and several books of your own. Inside these books are inspiring stories of God's faithfulness in the lives of your parents and you. His faithfulness when your car tire blew out, when your water heater died, when your air conditioner broke, when you lost your wallet, when you lost your wedding ring, when your baby's fever broke, when your dog got out, when your headache was healed, and more. They aren't someone's stories you've never met. They are your personal stories reinforcing the same thing over and over.

God is with you. God is for you. God has been faithful. God will always be faithful.

Ask yourself if such books would encourage you that whatever challenges you are facing are in God's hands. Now, ask yourself what a chronicle of the BIG stories would do for our faith and our children's faith.

BEGIN A MARY ROUTINE, NOW!

Predetermine to chronicle, in real-time, whatever you think you hear or see from God. By being predetermined and prepared, you are saying to God, loud and clear, "I want you to direct my steps. I value your words. I will not keep you locked in my prayer closet. You do not have to fit into my schedule because I am prepared at all times to receive from you." The results will be amazing.

AN IMPORTANT NOTE

There is a time and place for everything in life. The proper place for the subject matter of this book is in concert with a healthy Christian lifestyle. While a book many times larger than this could be written about a healthy Christian lifestyle, I regard the bare essentials as reading the bible, prayer, being in community with a group of believers, receiving instruction and receiving correction.

The whole point of this book is that we should not do all of the above and then put God in the narrow box of interacting with us only during the time when we are in our prayer closet. Life is a precious gift which should be lived with God by our side every moment.

How can we do so much to know God and become one with him, just to be caught up in The Big Gray Swirl *of life and not enjoy the rich interactions with God in the midst of our day? How can we not capture and treasure every interaction with God?*

Whether you are a student, stay home parent, doctor, lawyer, teacher, business man/woman etc., it only takes a few seconds to chronicle the faithfulness of God while walking to the car or during a coffee break or in between meetings or classes. Then on your day of rest you can remember them, elaborate on them and meditate on them.

I can imagine the blessing and feeling of security brought forth by having a full financial bank account. I cannot begin to imagine the blessing and security brought forth by having a full spiritual faith bank.

When my great-great-grand-children are my age, I want them to be free of The Big Gray Swirl *and have five generations of books, full of God's faithfulness next to their bibles.*

Chapter 8

Practical Suggestions and Coaching

Before publishing this book I sent out copies, of what I hoped was my final draft, for feedback and comments by proof readers. I was fascinated by the answers to one question. The question was, "Grade how well the book provided practical, helpful suggestions?" The grades were not consistent. I thought, "How can one person give it an "A" and another a "D?" Even though there are many ideas and suggestions sown throughout this book, I came to realize it would be helpful to consolidate some suggestions in this chapter.

Having said that, it also became evident that some people had wounds and hurts so deep, it was difficult for them to even accept the notion that God is faithful. One proof reader asked me, "So where was God when my mother's boyfriend attacked me?" and, "If I get free then what, more of the same junk?" So I will address both emotional wounds and give some coaching tips for a plan of action.

EMOTIONAL WOUNDS

It can be really hard to believe God is faithful when we are hurting. We need to be healed from emotional trauma to fully engage in the life God has for us. I so wish I could, through this book, remove the deep *emotional* wounds of death, sickness, neglect, abuse, assault, disappointment, poverty or any number of other terrible things. I spent years trying to help hurting people who would ask, "WHY?", with only an *intellectual* approach. So many times, I would have a good conversation, starting from how sin entered the world with Adam and Eve, then free-will and the terribly consequences of sin, all the way to Jesus, the gospels and the epistles, just for the person to thank me and come back a week later asking, "WHY?." Although a sound theological understanding of why bad things happen is important, sometimes we just need to be healed. If you think you need emotional healing, please talk to your pastor and get some guidance.

Even after we are healed, I know how hard it can be to stay thankful, positive and hopeful. I need an infusion of hope from time to time, a reminder of the beauty of God and His Gospel. We all need emotional and spiritual encouragement at times.

In addition to what my church offers, one of the websites I turn to is, LifeWithoutLimbs. org. There you will find the story and videos of Nick Vujicic, (pronounced: Vooy-cheech). He has a true gift for infusing hope, encouragement and leading people into a deep relationship with Christ. A song I've turned to regularly is, Jesus Lover of My Soul, by Hosanna Music. John G. Elliott has a series of 4 instrumental albums he calls soaking music. They are fantastic for prayer and meditation. Two of the most powerful movies I've ever seen about trusting God, asking why and forgiveness vs. hate, is Amish Grace and Soul Surfer. They are both true stories! Professional surfer Bethany Hamilton lives by faith and refuses to live in self-pity.

I also like to read the full 1937 seren-ity prayer as written by Reinhold Niebuhr. It reads, *Father, give us courage to change what must be altered, serenity to accept what cannot be helped, and the insight to know the one from the other. Living one day at a time; Enjoying one moment at a time; Accepting hardships as the pathway to peace; Taking, as He did, this sinful world as it is, not as I would have it; Trusting that He will make all things right if I surrender to His Will; That I may be reasonably happy in this life and supremely happy with Him Forever in the next. Amen.*

CHRONICLING NOT JOURNALING

When I speak of chronicling as opposed to jour-naling, I'm speaking of the real time capturing of our experiences. Journaling presupposes we will remember all of the details and intricacies of what we've seen or experienced. The issue is not losing, among the busyness and distractions of life, those memories which can only be re-called if prompted. You can journal and be total-ly unaware of what you forgot and what nuances of your experiences fell between the cracks.

It is important to immediately chronicle what occurs while it is still fresh and clear. Whether you fully chronicle an event or just a few words to prompt your memory later, it must be in real time.

COACHING TIPS

Do only one thing at a time as much as possible. If you're going to play a board game, just play a board game.

I was playing Battleship with my eight year-old son and watching a TV show. I caught myself being distracted, turned off the show and we played again. This time I paid attention to how he was playing and gave him some tips on how to play better. A week later he was playing his 18 year-old sister as she was multi-tasking and he beat her. He couldn't wait to tell me and I was the smartest dad ever because I chose to give him my undivided attention.

If you multiply the concept of being fully present vs. multi-tasking across your entire life, day after day, allowing God to speak into your most seemingly trivial activities it will improve the richness of your life enormously. This level of attentiveness may seem unattainable but let me encourage you; little by little you can do it.

Just drive. At most have your radio on. This is prime time to reflect back on your day, think ahead about your day and talk to God. I have a friend who continually makes calls when she's driving so she doesn't waste that time. I ask her, "How is talking to God while you're driving a waste of time?"

So many times I have a list of people I feel I need to call and touch base with. During a car trip talking to God, I'll get a sense of peace about not needing to call some of them. This gives me some of my time back. I've gotten pretty good at letting God show me who needs a call and who doesn't.

Even when on carpooling duty, I really try to be fully present, listening to what the kids are saying, being calm and giving God an opportunity to give me insights. The old way I was just trying to get from one place to the other, hearing nothing but a bunch of chattering kids, taking a phone call along the way and finally yelling, "Hey! You kids wanna hold it down? I'm on the phone!"

Just breathe. When I go through a really stressful season I use a little trick to stay clam and invite God in. I went to the pet store and bought a bag of small, smooth, aquarium rocks. Each morning I put five rocks in my pocket. When I start my day I take a pebble out of my pocket and put it in a glass bowl. I sit back in a chair, breathe in deeply for five seconds and breathe out for five seconds. At the end of each breath I say, "God is in control." I do this six times. It takes 60 seconds. Two hours into my day I do it again. At lunch I do it a third time. Two hours later I do it a fourth time. At the end of my day before dinner, I do it the fifth time.

This helps me stay calm and trust God. It also lowers my blood pressure and improves cognitive processing. A small glass bowl of rocks at my desk is a visual reminder to stay calm and to also trust God.

If you visit my site, www.GodImBusy.com, I'll give you a one-minute audio clip of the breathing exercise. I prompt you when to inhale and exhale. It's much better than trying to keep track of the time yourself and I add other encouraging phrases.

Together we can elevate God to a whole new level in our lives. We can hear clearer, be more intimate and allow God to direct our steps more specifically.

The important thing about recognizing some-thing worth chronicling is not to over think things. This will be a lifelong process of tuning into the voice of God during the midst of your day. A process of letting God out of your prayer closet and inviting God along in everything you do. Each one of us is different, so how much of a prompt you will need is different. Writing too little or too much, will work itself out if you just keep chronicling and don't let it become an obligatory burden.

In terms of how you choose to chronicle, the important thing is to pick something you'll actually use. I'm a big fan of a small pocket notebook and a digital voice recorder. I can keep them in my briefcase, backpack or pocket. I use the notebook for the short prompts and the recorder for the longer ones.

The key to success is simplicity and ease of use. If it isn't simple and easy for you to use, find a method that is.

Chapter 9

The Conclusion of the Whole Matter

Your life matters because you matter. God created you beautifully and wonderfully. You don't have to rush through life, busy and distracted just to fade away when your time here is done.

Your stories matter because you matter. Your stories of victories won and hardships overcome should strengthen you not wear you down and make you bitter.

You should be free from busyness to find your calling in life and your life-lessons should be passed on and celebrated for generations to come.

You may need to read this book several times to incorporate it into your life. That's a small price to pay so you can get to the place where you simply enjoy the experience of life, rather than rushing though it in *The Big Gray Swirl*.

Start with whatever you have on hand. I started with a little notebook and it worked for me and others. Just calm down, look for the hand of God, invite Him into the midst of your day and chronicle your experiences so you won't forget them and aren't tempted to start rushing around and multi-tasking again.

God will redeem the time. God will direct your steps. God will keep you focused. You have time to fulfill the purposes of God in your life while enjoying the struggle of the journey!

Your children and your children's children, want and need your stories of God's faithfulness.

You can do it! God bless you.

Appendix One

A Few Scriptures about the
Faithfulness of God
(God's Word translation)

I'm not worthy of all the love and faithfulness you have shown me. I only had a shepherd's staff when I crossed the Jordan River, but now I have two camps.
(Genesis 32:10)

O LORD, your mercy reaches to the heavens, your faithfulness to the skies.
(Psalms 36:5)

I have not buried your righteousness deep in my heart. I have been outspoken about your faithfulness and your salvation. I have not hidden your mercy and your truth from those assembled for worship.
(Psalms 40:10)

Because of your faithfulness, O my God, even I will give thanks to you as I play on a lyre. I will make music with a harp to praise you, O Holy One of Israel.
(Psalms 71:22)

Will anyone tell about your mercy in Sheol or about your faithfulness in Abaddon?
(Psalms 88:11)

I will sing forever about the evidence of your mercy, O LORD. I will tell about your faithfulness to every generation.
(Psalms 89:1)

I said, "Your mercy will last forever. Your faithfulness stands firm in the heavens."
(Psalms 89:2)

O LORD, the heavens praise your miracles and your faithfulness in the assembly of the holy ones.
(Psalms 89:5)

O LORD God of Armies, who is like you? Mighty LORD, even your faithfulness surrounds you.
(Psalms 89:8)

My faithfulness and mercy will be with him, and in my name He will be victorious.
(Psalms 89:24)

Where is the evidence of your mercy, Lord? You swore an oath to David on the basis of your faithfulness.
(Psalms 89:49)

It is good to announce your mercy in the morning and your faithfulness in the evening
(Psalms 92:2)

The LORD is good. His mercy endures forever. His faithfulness endures throughout every generation.
(Psalms 100:5)

Don't give glory to us, O LORD. Don't give glory to us. Instead, give glory to your name because of your mercy and faithfulness.
(Psalms 115:1)

His mercy toward us is powerful. The LORD'S faithfulness endures forever. Hallelujah!
(Psalms 117:2)

I have chosen a life of faithfulness. I have set your regulations in front of me.
(Psalms 119:30)

Your faithfulness endures throughout every generation. You set the earth in place, and it continues to stand.
(Psalms 119:90)

By mercy and faithfulness, peace is made with the LORD. By the fear of the LORD, evil is avoided.
(Proverbs 16:6)

Justice will be the belt around His waist. Faithfulness will be the belt around His hips.
(Isaiah 11:5)

Those who are living praise you as I do today. Fathers make your faithfulness known to their children.
(Isaiah 38:19)

It is new every morning. His faithfulness is great.
(Lamentations 3:23)

What if some of them were unfaithful? Can their unfaithfulness cancel God's faithfulness?
(Romans 3:3)

But the spiritual nature produces love, joy, peace, patience, kindness, goodness, faithfulness . . .
(Galatians 5:22)

Appendix Two

Testimonies of Escaping The Big Gray Swirl

Linda and **Lee Kane** are a devoted couple with children, grandchildren, a business and many responsibilities. I met Linda and Lee through a mutual friend. I knew they had a lot on their plate, but had no idea until I received this testimony.

This is Linda's story of freedom from *The Big Gray Swirl*.

On Thursday Lee and I were up by three am to travel home from Canada after a long two week trip. After a three hour lay over in Seattle, a little necessary shopping, visiting with our friends who met us at the airport and a very late lunch we finally made it home by early evening. We were met by stacks of mail, packages and phone messages. By evening we fell into bed exhausted.

Friday morning started with paperwork, emails and a conference call. Then a quick trip to the bank was needed to avert a potential problem, grocery shopping, a stop at the dairy and signing some paperwork which needed to be done a week ago. Somehow lunch got missed, not always uncommon. Friday evening our son and his family came by. Lee needed help cutting down a Cherry tree which was dying. I was weeding the rock parkways and putting my stepping stones back out after being in the garage all winter. We were enjoying spending time with our kids and before we knew it, it was eight thirty and we were quickly ordering pizza for dinner.

Saturday morning Lee and I were up early to finish weeding the parkways. Then I was off to do five evaluations, while Lee took off to soccer games and later laying sod in our yard. I got home about seven pm, just before our three granddaughters came over to spend time with Papa and Grandma. The two older girls were staying for a sleep over. In the back of my mind I am trying to figure out when our grandsons could have their turn for a sleep over, too. Grandchildren time is extremely precious and important. By ten thirty the littlest one got picked up and we are helping with teeth brushing and getting the other two into bed. God, I'm too busy!!!

Sunday morning I am up before seven. Hopefully the girls will sleep late. I really wanted to have some quiet. Before I could even sit down, everyone was up and wanting breakfast.

Welcome to a picture of our world for the past twelve or more years. It has been a continual going from one project, commitment or event to another. Never having enough time to do everything and never, ever getting caught up. I knew we were walking in our calling. We work with families with children from gifted to severely disabled. While this is a passion and we are so grateful we do what we do, it is also stressful. There are desperate and heartbreaking situations we work with all the time.

After reading Alan's book, I began to really look at the craziness and business of our lives.

In the past when people would ask me how I do what I do, I would simply tell them I did not think about it. I just did it. Now, I really began to think about it. Last month we were in and out of six different hotels or houses during our three week trip to Texas. I was done. I was fried. I was so tired of living out of suit cases. I was so tired with lugging things in and packing them out. I was really fed up with airports and what traveling 250+ days per year entailed.

Two years ago Lee had suggested we buy a motor home and drive everywhere we go. Suddenly, this sounded like the perfect solution. I instantly had peace with this idea. We only had three days home before leaving for Canada. If we were going to find an RV, it would have to be during those three days. We began to earnestly pray. Lord, is this your plan? We heard Him say yes.

Our first thought was to buy something used. We scoured the online classifieds. That really did not seem the way to go. At the first dealership the salesman barely gave us the time of day. It was almost as if he did not want to show us RV's. It was time to go. The second dealership was totally different. The salesman took us into his office and wanted to hear what our needs were. He wanted to know what we were looking for and how we would use it. He was totally tuned in to us. He started showing us some used models. The more we talked, though, the more he said he felt we were looking at the wrong type of motor home. And, he happened to have an RV whose sale just had fallen through that day. He felt it was the perfect home for us, with an incredible price.

As we left the dealership that night, we started praying. This was such a huge decision and we needed to hear from the Lord. I distinctly heard the Lord say, "You asked. I delivered."

That evening I searched the internet. I read articles. I looked for hours for that motor home at a cheaper price. No one came even close. We were convinced this was indeed the motor home the Lord had set aside for us.

Through driving where we need to go, I see hours and hours of time opened up to me. Time I can spend with the Lord, in Bible study, working, writing a book I need to write and countless other things which would be lost to the business and craziness of life. I see our pace slowing down and stress dissipating. I see the change of life the Lord told me would come.

Reading about Alan's vision for chronicling exchanges with God and His faithfulness, I got so very excited. How I would have loved to have had my Grandmother's stories written down. How I would love to have my parent's stories chronicled. How I would love to leave a legacy of encouragement for my children and grandchildren. Alan's vision for doing such is absolutely incredible. It is the tool for preserving our stories and increasing our relationship with the Lord. I can not wait for the vision to come to pass so we can all participate with and reap the benefits of the vision. I pray for the finances to overflow so it comes to fruition quickly.

Mindy **Wood** is a wife, mom, professional writer and teacher. I met Mindy Wood while looking for a writer to help edit and polish this book. I found her experience and insight indispensable and she found the concepts of this book life-changing.

This is Mindy's story of freedom from *The Big Gray Swirl*.

I sat in a puddle of tears as I whispered a sincere prayer, "God don't let me pass from this life without doing what You created me to do." No I wasn't dying but felt somehow lost in a sea of demands, trapped in a cycle of doing instead of being. It seemed that one day was racing into the next and I was just living for living's sake instead of living with purpose.

As a writer and editor I live my life around planning and deadlines but as a busy mother, wife, career woman and home educator I find myself forgetting what this life is all about. I fit the profile of one seriously distracted woman, cell phone and laptop never far from my reach as I juggle a lot! So much for a purpose driven life.

Reading this book has taught me that I have to change my habits. If my schedule doesn't include quiet time with God at the end of the day or even enough time to jot down "God mail" messages during the day then my schedule needs to change. I check and return messages on my phone and laptop all day but I don't have time to check messages from God and reply? No wonder I was distraught that day and feeling lost in my busy life.

Since reading this, I've started taking charge of my schedule instead of my schedule running me. I jot those thoughts down and pay attention to the little things from God that interrupts my day. Finally I began to realize the things He was trying to show me for more than a year. Amazingly the course and focus of my life has changed very quickly and my purpose, once hidden, is beginning to emerge.

Thank God, He IS faithful!

Jan Bedell is a wife, mom, business owner and certified master neurodevelopmentalist. I met Jan years ago and she was and still is one of the busiest people I've known. I have consulted with Jan personally and professionally. The transformation she has gone through is nothing short of amazing.

This is Jan's story of freedom from *The Big Gray Swirl*.

I work with people who face mild to severe challenges in the way their brains function. I see children, teens and adults who have diagnosis as severe as cognitively challenged and autism to people with labels such as dyslexia and ADHD as well as those who simply want to improve their memory and mental function.

As a devout Christian I rely on God to speak to me. It wasn't until I was mentored by the ideas in Alan's book that I realized God was actually trying to speak to me in everyday situations, but I wasn't paying close enough attention to recognize it. In the past God has spoken to me through nature but that was typically when I was taking a walk, which I don't do enough, or when I am gardening, which is a hobby that I don't get to indulge in very often. These times are apparently when I "calm down" enough to really hear.

After a particularly busy week, a gardening encounter brought me to tears as God revealed his truths to me. I had planted seeds in small compartments of a 24-pack container for a vegetable garden a few weeks earlier. The seedlings standing tall and vying for sunlight in the green house delighted the eyes of this novice gardener. Then I realized that the small soil containers would not support the life of all the seedlings. I decided to transplant three or four of them into larger containers until the garden would be ready and the weather was co-operative. I started with zeal to carefully sepa-rate each seedling and place it in a cup which disrupted all the seedlings root balls. Then I thought, I don't have enough cups or potting soil for all of these to be transplanted and be-sides that, I don't have enough real estate in my small garden to put that many plants. That is when I started plucking out some of the seed-lings from each container to maintain the in-tegrity of one root ball per space. It was so very hard! The discarded plants were often just as tall as the one left in the soil. They were alive and had the potential for bearing fruit just like the other one if given a chance. Tears started flowing from my eyes as I realized what God was telling me. The seedlings were good but what was *best*? If I had left them all in the soil they would have choked each other out and there would have been no fruit at all; all the hard work of planting, watering . . . would have been lost.

I populated the garden with the seedlings and took the "rejects" back to the greenhouse. Some immediately entered the compost to become future fertilizer but some I just couldn't toss out. It actually was a good thing because the windy days that followed, killed several of the garden seedlings and the ones in the greenhouse had filled the container with strong roots and were already starting to bear fruit. You just never know when you put hopes and dreams on the shelf when they might reappear to bring a blessing.

Other lessons from this experience are too lengthy to detail here but suffice it to say that we only have so much real estate in life and if we overcrowd it, everything suffers. Thank you, Alan for teaching me about chronicling so I won't miss the answers God is providing for me and my business.

Appendix Three

A Vision of the Future

My passion is for you to escape *The Big Gray Swirl* of busyness and distractions to see the awesome faithfulness of God. My desire for you is to live a rich life immersed in each moment allowing God to direct your steps as you walk in your destiny.

I pray this book will help you and scores of others to be stronger in the faith.

Perhaps most important, your stories of your life-lessons, your victories and your accomplishments will become a legacy of faith to future generations. To come to fruition all that God has put on my heart, we will use technology as a tool for spiritual growth rather than spiritual decay.

THE SOLUTION I'VE ENVISIONED

I am creating an ultra secure and private online application which will allow you to phone, text message, email or log on and type your stories of God's faithfulness in your lives. I will integrate a simple word processing tool for editing your stories. You will be able to title your stories and put them into one chapter or multiple chapters. You will be able to create as many different chapters as you want. You will be able to search for stories using dozens of filters including words and terms you used in the story.

I want a 72 year-old to be able to search for stories they wrote 60 years earlier. I want that 72 year-old to be able to easily give their 12 year-old grandchild stories they wrote when they were 12 years-old.

The application will have a print-on-demand module, making it simple to select the stories you want for the particular book you are creating. You will be able to create books for yourselves and your children. You can create books of your stories with themes like, *Healing, Business, All the Little Things, The Children as Babies*, etc. In addition to being able to create books there will be the ability to create eBooks.

You will be able to push your stories out to other social network sites if you choose to. This way you only have to enter important stories in one place if you want to share them on other sites.

You will, also, have a prayer wall. Unlike Facebook or other social media sites, your prayer wall will be completely private and confidential. Your prayer wall can only be discovered and seen by your invitation, not others' requests. We will be able to pray for each other and encourage each other privately and securely.

There will be coaching tracks from many contributors.

1. A new member can choose to receive encouragement to escape *The Big Gray Swirl* and chronicle the faithfulness of God.

2. An expectant mother can choose to receive encouragement to chronicle their pregnancy and what they are hearing from God about their child.

3. New moms can receive encouragement to chronicle their child's growth during those first precious years.

4. Businessmen and women can receive encouragement to run a godly company and chronicle God's faithfulness in the process.

5. College students can receive encouragement to remain true to their faith and chronicle God's faithfulness.

6. High school students can receive encouragement to grow into the person God created them to be, while chronicling His faithfulness.

7. The opportunities for men and women of God to join with me and create coaching tracks are endless.

Staying Proactive

It's time to be proactive with how we utilize technology. We need to be committed to staying on top of emerging technologies so we decide how to best utilize them for the kingdom of God.

For example: I've been watching the development of video glasses for several years. Video glasses would allow you to view video sources privately through glasses. In the beginning they were big, heavy, ugly and expensive. As the technology has matured they have become more slim-line and attractive. You can even choose to look through the glasses, at the real world, or at the video display. If in the future they become the norm for reading eBooks, I will be prepared to incorporate the technology into how we read our stories of God's faithfulness. We must be confident that our stories will be read by future generations so they can stay free and stay strong in faith.

CONTACT THE AUTHOR

If you want to give me your thoughts about this book or have me to come and speak or feel you have a part in bringing the vision to fruition, please email me at AlanBias@ GodImBusy.com.

If you want to keep up-to-date with my speaking engagements or follow the developments of the online application visit me at www.GodImBusy.com.

I try to reach out about once a week through Twitter, Facebook and email. To follow me on Twitter simply text (Follow GodImBusy) to 40404. My Facebook page is www.FaceBook.com/GodImBusy.

To receive emails visit my website www. GodImBusy.com. Also, from the website you can soon find podcasts and other free offers. As our numbers grow we will post other members' tips on what they do to get free and stay free.